ONE SEA, ONE LAW?

By the same author

Seeing Through the Dark: Blind and Sighted—a Vision Shared

Why Glass Breaks, Rubber Bends, and Glue Sticks

BY MALCOLM E. WEISS

One Sea,

HARCOURT BRACE JOVANOVICH, PUBLISHERS

One Law?

THE FIGHT FOR A LAW OF THE SEA

Illustrated with photographs

SAN DIEGO NEW YORK LONDON

All metric equivalents are approximate figures.

Requests for permission to make copies of any part of the work should be mailed to: Permissions, Harcourt Brace Jovanovich, Publishers, 757 Third Avenue, New York, New York 10017.

Printed in the United States of America

LIBRARY OF CONGRESS CATALOGING IN PUBLICATION DATA
Weiss, Malcolm E. One sea, one law?
Bibliography: p. Includes index.
SUMMARY: Discusses the food, mineral, and energy sources the sea holds for mankind and the need for international law to ensure that these sources are not exploited, polluted, or wasted.
1. Maritime law—Juvenile literature. 2. Marine resources conservation—Law and legislation—Juvenile literature. 3. Marine resources—Juvenile literature. [1. Maritime law. 2. Marine resources conservation. 3. Marine resources] I. Title.
JX4419.W44 341.4'5 81-47535
ISBN 0-15-258690-3 AACR2

B C D E FIRST EDITION

Contents

One TROUBLE FOR OILED WATERS 1

Two HOW THE LAW OF THE SEA BEGAN 13

Three THERE IS ONE OCEAN 19

Four EXPLORING THE SEA, FROM MAURY TO THE PRESENT 32

Five FISHING THE SEA 48

Six DOWN IN THE FARM 59

Seven THE TREASURES OF THE SEA 73

Eight POLLUTION: MEDITERRANEAN PEACEMAKER, WORLD PROBLEM 87

CONTENTS

Nine WHAT LAW FOR THE SEA? 97

Ten RATIFICATION OR REJECTION? 107

BIBLIOGRAPHY 111

INDEX 116

ONE SEA, ONE LAW?

Chapter 1 TROUBLE FOR OILED WATERS

As the 1980s opened, the biggest oil spill in the world's history was going on. It was a grand beginning for a time of energy shortages. As revelers rang in the new year, oil from a damaged well was gushing into the Gulf of Mexico at a rate of more than 14,000 gallons (53,000 liters) an hour.

But that was nothing new. The oil had been gushing for half a year by then, sometimes at three times that rate—about 1,000,000 gallons (3,785,000 liters) in twenty-four hours.

It had started on a day in June. The crew on the platform of Ixtoc I sweltered in the tropical heat, 24 miles (38.6 kilometers) off the coast of southern Mexico. Far below the platform, the drill shaft of Ixtoc I probed thousands of feet into the seabed of the Gulf of Mexico.

The floor of the gulf has yielded up rich oil finds before. On that June day, Ixtoc's drill shaft struck one of the richest—an undersea oil field containing perhaps 33.6 billion barrels of oil. At the rate the United States uses oil today, that would take care of this country's oil needs for about four and a half years.

Oil isn't found in big underground pools. Instead the oil is spread out in droplets between the grains of porous rocks like sandstone. In some places the oil is under enormous pressure from the natural gas that has formed with it. This is so at Ixtoc. Usually a cap of fine-grained rock lies over the oil field. These are natural lids that keep the oil from spouting upward.

When the drill shaft of such an oil well breaks through the cap rock, oil and gas surge up through the shaft with tremendous force. Only what oilmen call drilling "mud" holds them back. The "mud" is a mixture of clay, water, and chemicals pumped down through the drill shaft. It is used to lubricate and cool the shaft, bearing away some of the heat produced by drilling. It is also used to keep oil and gas from geysering up the shaft when oil or gas under high pressure is struck.

But sometimes the "mud" drains into the porous rock that holds the oil. That's what happened at Ixtoc I.

Suddenly, the "mud" stopped circulating. It was a warning of trouble ahead.

Normally, the first thing to do under such circumstances is to start pumping still heavier "mud" down the shaft. But there wasn't enough on hand to pump, so the crew tried pumping seawater. It didn't work. Nor did an attempt to cut through the drill shaft and cap it. Hot oil and gas erupted up the shaft, exploding into flame in the open air.

In fact, nothing seemed to work. A crew brought in from the United States couldn't stop the runaway well either. Seven weeks later, oil in enormous quantities was still pouring into the Gulf of Mexico. The oil, lighter than water, rose to the surface. In the summer months, there is a strong flow of water northwestward across the gulf. By July, streamers of oil, some 300 miles (482.7 kilometers) long, stretched from the site of Ixtoc I toward the coast of Texas. In some places it formed a thin rainbow-colored slick on the ocean surface. In others, it was thick, gluey, brown, and foul-smelling.

The spreading oil threatened Texas beaches, including the Padre Island National Seashore, a nesting ground for some 350 species of birds and a large variety of other animals. It threatened resort areas and rich shrimp-fishing grounds.

Summer passed and fall came. By the start of October, oil slicks were being sighted in many parts of the gulf. There was fear the slicks might get as far as the Florida Keys off the southern tip of mainland Florida.

As the season changed, the flow of water in the gulf shifted from northward to southward, moving the oil away from the Texas coast. Now it was damaging the shrimp fisheries along the Mexican coast.

Some 110,000 two-inch-wide (5.1-centimeter) metal balls were pumped down the drill shaft of Ixtoc I in an attempt to slow the flood of oil. The balls, about 80,000 of lead and 30,000 of steel, were to slow down the upward rush of oil and gas by friction. As the rush slowed, the balls would sink farther toward the bottom, eventually cutting off most of the flow.

That was the idea, but it didn't work either. Fall is a time of storms and high winds in the gulf, and the hose used to pump the balls into the shaft broke. Rough seas, driven by hurricane winds, broke the hinges on a 310-ton (281-metric-ton) steel cone meant to cap Ixtoc.

By mid-October, Ixtoc was still gushing at a rate of 18,000 gallons (68,000 liters) an hour. By the time the well was capped, in March, about 150,000,000 gallons (568,000,000 liters) of oil had been spilled.

But before then, another major oil spill had taken place in the gulf. On November 1, the oil tanker *Burmah Agate* collided with the freighter *Mimosa* in clear weather and calm seas. The tanker burned for five weeks. Eleven million of its 16,000,000-gallon (60,600,000-liter) cargo poured into the gulf just off the shore of Galveston, Texas, where the collision took place.

Coincidence? Bad luck?

Not really. About 1,250 supertanker cargoes pass through the Caribbean Sea and the Gulf of Mexico each year. These ships carry 71.4 *billion* (270.2 billion liters) gallons of oil and oil-related products, such as natural gas.

In fact, the people living in the gulf area—both American and Mexican—have been lucky. Much of the 11,000,000 gallons (41,600,000 liters) spilled from the tanker was carried away from Galveston Bay and the

A United States plane, tracking the oil spill from Ixtoc in the Gulf of Mexico in August 1979, casts its shadow over a long oil slick that is coming ashore on a Mexican beach 60 miles (96.5 kilometers) south of Brownsville, Texas. A few days later the oil came ashore at Brownsville itself. (NOAA)

shallows where shellfish and other food animals spawn. And most of the 150,000,000 gallons (568,000,000 liters) of oil spewed into the Gulf of Mexico by Ixtoc I did not end up on the beaches and coastal islands of the United States or Mexico.

But the long-term damage may be harder to measure. One thing the Ixtoc oil spill proved is that oil pollution lasts a long time in tropical waters.

The polluting oil forms an emulsion with the seawater. The oil spreads evenly through the water in tiny droplets, much as droplets of cream are spread through homogenized milk. At the Ixtoc site, the oil-water emulsion covering the sea was 60 percent water and 40 percent oil. After the slicks had drifted some 600 miles (965.6 kilometers) northward to the Texas coast, the emulsion was not much changed; it was 70 percent water and 30 percent oil. So after drifting hundreds of miles over a period of ten weeks, the oil was not much diluted.

Oil spills can have a disastrous effect on wildlife. Oil can kill an animal or a plant quickly by coating it and sealing it off from oxygen. It can also kill slowly because it readily dissolves pesticides and other poisons, which are then absorbed by living things. It can kill in more hidden ways. Small amounts of oil absorbed by a fish, bird, or other animal can lower its resistance to disease and make it weaker. Even animals that are not killed can be harmed by a spill. Oil contains powerful cancer-causing substances that make edible shellfish like clams, oysters, scallops, and mussels inedible.

This much and more we know about the short-term effects of oil pollution. But John Robinson, manager of hazardous materials response for the National Oceanic and Atmospheric Administration (NOAA), says we know surprisingly little about the long-term effects of oil on the environment.

Mr. Robinson says the large population of birds that nest on the south Texas coast has gone down by as much as 50 percent since the Ixtoc spill. Much of the sea life off the beaches has been killed. Recovery seems very slow. The ocean floor near the coast is littered with large tar mats—sticky masses produced by chemical reactions between the oil and seawater. These mats may last for years, the toxic substances in them slowly spreading out through the surrounding water. We do not know what damage this may do to life in the sea. But we do know that the eggs and young forms of many sea animals live in or on the sea floor.

Mr. Robinson says it will take several years to find out the full effect of the spill on Texas beaches. And Dr. Eric Schneider, professor of ocean management at the University of Rhode Island, says, "Ixtoc will probably have the largest environmental effect man has had on the oceans yet."

But at least the damage done by the Ixtoc oil spill can be measured. Who will pay for the damage and for cleaning up is a much harder question to answer.

At first thought the answer seems simple. The polluter is at fault. The polluter should pay the costs.

But who is the polluter in this case? Is it the Mexican government, which operates Ixtoc and owns the offshore oil in this part of the gulf? Or is it the United States company that leased the drilling equipment to Mexico? The company may have leased faulty equipment or otherwise been negligent.

It was because of these possibilities that the state of

Texas sued *both* the United States leasing company and the Mexican government for damages. That shows how difficult it is to say clearly who was at fault in the Ixtoc oil spill. As we shall see later on, there is usually no simple answer to the problem of responsibility for pollution at sea.

In fact, there are very few laws that restrict any use that may be made of the deep sea. By the same token, the laws limiting or controlling pollution in the deep sea are few and vague.

When we talk about the "deep sea" or the "deep seabed" or the "high seas," we mean the parts of the sea beyond the control of any nation. For centuries, countries have claimed control of navigation and fishing rights in a band of ocean waters around their coasts. This is the territorial sea.

By long tradition, nations have accepted a three-mile (4.8-kilometer) limit for the territorial sea. That goes back to the old English Cannon Shot Rule of 1737. Three miles, according to the lawyers who made the rule, was as far as a cannon could shoot in those days.

The lawyers were wrong. No cannon could shoot that far in 1737. Of course since then weapons have become much more powerful. And mineral wealth, such as oil, has been discovered in coastal waters. Science has created the means of finding and using this wealth. So nations have expanded the size of their claims to a territorial sea. More than fifty nations now claim a 12-mile (19.3-kilometer) limit to their coastal waters. Others, including the United States, claim rights out to 200 miles (321.8 kilometers).

However, even 200 miles is a short distance compared to the vastness of the sea. And beyond the limits of the coastal waters, no law applies except the old doctrine of freedom of the seas.

At least that was true through 1980. But on November 1, 1967, a struggle to make a rule of law for the high seas began. It started with a now famous speech in the United Nations General Assembly.

The speaker was Dr. Arvid Pardo. At the time, he was the ambassador of Malta to the United Nations. Dr. Pardo called for a set of laws for the high seas. The law he proposed would extend to the depths of the sea, to the seabed itself, and beneath the seabed, where much mineral wealth lies.

Dr. Pardo pointed out that there were vast resources of mineral wealth in the sea. Man's science and technology were now putting those riches within his grasp.

But to whom did those riches belong? On this question, what law there was, was silent. The laws of the sea were far behind the times. No nation owned the great expanse of the deep-sea floor.

Yet a handful of nations now has the power to mine the treasures that lay on and beneath the floor of the deep seabed. With no laws but the old idea of freedom of the seas, the answer to the question "Who owns this wealth?" has to be "First come, first served."

The sea is too deep for old laws. Ambassador Pardo foresaw a race to carve up the resources of the seabed. And a race is not won by care but by speed. The seabed might be carved up with no care for the pollution it might cause and with little concern for any threat to the complex chain of life in the oceans. There might even be a war between major powers quarreling over mining rights to some part of the ocean.

This would repeat the history of what man has done on dry land. Does it need to be repeated? It has been a wasteful history—wasteful of energy, wasteful of the land's priceless gifts of food and mineral wealth, and wasteful of lives.

Ambassador Pardo proposed to the General Assembly that some kind of international law be set up for the sea before such exploitation began. He suggested that the seabed and its resources be declared "the common heritage of mankind." Coastal states claim for themselves the sea and the land beneath it out to a certain distance. So Pardo said the UN should work out a treaty among its members to define the limits of national rights regarding the seabed. Beyond those limits would lie the international seabed, "the common heritage of mankind."

Pardo made clear what he meant by the idea of a common heritage. The resources of the seabed and the wealth derived from those resources were to be used for the benefit of all countries and all people. The international seabed could be used only for peaceful purposes. There could be no weapons in or on the sea floor.

On that last point, some progress has been made. Both the United States and the Soviet Union put forward ideas for a treaty to bar weapons from the seabed. By 1971, a treaty prohibiting nuclear weapons and "other weapons of mass destruction" from the seabed was written and was signed by sixty-two nations, including the United States and the Union of Soviet Socialist Republics.

Since then, work on a law of the sea has gone very slowly. Part of the reason is mutual suspicion and distrust among nations.

There are other reasons. Any workable law of the sea is going to have to deal with a lot of problems—over a lot of water. The oceans cover almost three-quarters of our planet.

The law of the sea will have to regulate fishing over all that vast area. It may have to regulate aquaculture—the growing of ocean plants and animals for food. Aquaculture is a very old art. In the future, it will become more and more important as a source of food for everyone on earth. In addition, one of a law of the sea's most important jobs will be to regulate mining the sea for oil, gas, and metal ores.

The sea holds great promise for mankind—the promise of plentiful food for the world and of new sources of minerals and energy to help build and run factories and machines. Whether the promise will be fulfilled depends on how wisely we use the sea. The writing and signing of a treaty on the law of the sea is a first step toward the wise use of the sea.

The need for such a treaty has grown over many hundreds of years. It has grown as our understanding of the sea has grown. It has grown with our power to use the sea and its riches.

This book is the story of that growth. It begins thousands of years ago, when the first law of the sea was put down in writing. It was a simple law. Since the people of that time had little power over the sea or in it, there was no need for complex laws.

The book ends with the struggle to create a new law of the sea. Final agreement on that law is important. It is a test of our willingness to work together to make the sea in fact the common heritage of mankind.

Chapter 2 HOW THE LAW OF THE SEA BEGAN

Our story begins with the oldest highways used by man. They were made of water. The great rivers have been natural highways for thousands—perhaps millions—of years.

In the language of ancient Egypt, there were but two ways to say "I travel." One was "I sail upstream"; the other, "I sail downstream." And doubtless long before that, some lazy and inventive cave dweller climbed on a floating log and took a free ride down a river.

The oceans were too vast to be crossed by floating logs: too vast, too stormy, and too unpredictable. Besides, prehistoric people must have assumed that the oceans had no end. That is why, in many myths, the world is an island surrounded by an endless sea.

Although cave dwellers could not cross the sea, they often chose to live near it. There are many caves around the Mediterranean Sea, for example, that are now 200 or 300 feet (61 or 91.4 meters) under water. In Stone Age times, these caves were on the shore. As the last Ice Age passed, the huge caps of ice around the North and South poles slowly melted, adding enormous quantities of water to the seas. Around the world, sea levels rose. Shorelines flooded, and caves once on dry land became underwater homes for fish, lobsters, crabs, and eels.

In our own times, people have returned to these caves, looking for the story of their pasts. Archaeologists have put on diving suits and taken their picks and axes and their scientific methods beneath the sea.

Beneath the floors of these flooded caves lie the records of thousands of years of human life. There are tools and bones and the remains of plants.

Some of the bones found are fish bones. In fact, the first people to find a seashore must have soon found that a meal could be made of the many animals easily gathered from the sea. A million years ago early Stone Age man made bone harpoons for spearing fish. Later, bone hooks, nets, and fishing boats were invented.

With the invention of boats, something that can be called a science of the sea must have started. People began to watch for signs of dangerous storms. They discovered the cycle of the tides. They learned more about the animals and plants of the coastal oceans. As they traveled farther out to sea, they began to use the stars for navigation.

At first, this knowledge was not written down. It was passed on from generation to generation by word of mouth, sometimes "coded" into elaborate myths.

The first written record of the science of the sea was

made by Aristotle in the fourth century B.C. He wrote careful descriptions of 180 different kinds of sea animals.

Over the next five hundred years, some of that knowledge seems to have been lost. In the first century A.D., Pliny "the Elder" wrote his 37 volumes of natural history and mentioned 176 different species of marine animal life.

Pliny didn't know that he had "lost" four species. What's more, he was quite confident that he had listed every ocean animal there was. "Everyone knows," he wrote, "that it is quite impossible to comprise every species of terrestrial animal in one general view for the information of mankind. And yet, by Hercules! in the sea . . . vast as it is, there exists nothing that is unknown to us, and, a truly marvelous fact, it is with those things that Nature has concealed in the deep that we are best acquainted!"

He was wrong, dead wrong. He was so far off that his error seems comical. But we should not be too ready to laugh. The mistake of believing that all is known about a subject and nothing remains to be discovered is the most common of human errors. It has been made by all sorts of people at all times throughout history.

Nevertheless, Pliny's writings were immensely valuable. They were one of the few bits of wisdom to survive through the Middle Ages and give a foundation of learning to the Renaissance.

Of course, in Pliny's day, the idea of science as an organized body of knowledge subject to constant revision did not exist, so his flat statement that there were no new and unknown animals to be found in the sea does not sound so odd.

Long before Pliny or Aristotle, of course, real exploration of the oceans had begun. One of the earliest recorded was the voyage, around 1500 B.C., of Queen Hatshepsut of ancient Egypt through the Red Sea and the Gulf of Aden to what is now Somalia.

By 1500 B.C., the Egyptians had been building well-designed boats for three thousand years or more—not surprising since the main highway of Egypt was the Nile. In many ways, the Nile is still the most important road in Egypt.

The ships of Queen Hatshepsut's fleet were each about 70 feet (21.3 meters) long. They were powered by oars and sails and built to travel swiftly for their day. They were trading ships, carrying gum, incense, ebony, ivory, gold, and assorted live animals and animal skins.

By 500 B.C., the great sea-going traders of the ancient world, the Phoenicians, claimed to have sailed around the southern tip of Africa. Most of the sailors of their time thought that was just a tall story. For one thing, the Phoenicians said that as they sailed from east to west around the southernmost point of Africa, the noon sun was to their right. In other words, the noon sun was in the north. And everyone knew that the noon sun's direction is southerly. It should have been to their left.

It is just this detail in their account that made the Phoenician claim believable to later generations, for if they sailed where they said, the Phoenicians were far south of the equator. And there the noon sun *would* have been on their right. The people of that time living north of the equator did not know that.

These early sailors took samples from the sea floor where it was shallow. They had learned to tell deep water from shallow water by the kinds of waves, the color of the sea, and by many other signs.

Over the next nineteen hundred years, ships grew in size. They changed to great sailing vessels and then to steam-powered ships. But in all that time, not much more was learned about the sea and its ways than had been known by the ancients.

During all this time, the seas were major highways for trade, as they still are. About four thousand years ago, a king of Babylonia, Hammurabi, set down a book of laws called the Code of Hammurabi. The Babylonians were a seafaring people, and the code established a law of the sea.

It was a simple law, reflecting the fact that the oceans were highways. Like any roads, the seas should be free to trade. Freedom of the sea was freedom to navigate the sea, and it was a right possessed by all who could build and sail ships.

Over and over again, this same idea was expressed as law by many people. In the 1500s, Ivan the Terrible, Czar of Russia, called the oceans "God's road." Queen Elizabeth I of England rejected Spanish complaints about English "pirates" attacking Spanish treasure ships. "The use of the sea and the air is common to all," she answered. "Neither can title to the ocean belong to any people or private person. . . ."

One Sea, One Law?

In 1609, a twenty-six-year-old Dutch lawyer, Hugo Grotius, wrote a treatise called *Mare Liberum* (Freedom of the Sea). He appealed "to the civilized world for complete freedom of the high seas for the innocent use and mutual benefit of all." Grotius wrote, "The sea is common to all, because it is so limitless that it cannot become a possession of anyone and because it is adapted for the use of all."

Ringing words, and clear. But battles were also fought on the sea. And then, as now, nations declared the freedom of the seas with one voice—and claimed vast tracts of the trackless sea for themselves with another.

Chapter 3 THERE IS ONE OCEAN

"There is a river in the ocean. In the severest droughts it never fails, and in the mightiest floods it never overflows. Its banks and bottoms are of cold water, while its current is of warm. The Gulf of Mexico is its fountain, and its mouth is the Arctic Sea. It is the Gulf Stream."

That is the way a textbook on the science of the oceans —oceanography—begins. Textbooks, especially modern ones, are not usually written in such a colorful style. But this book, *The Physical Geography of the Sea,* was written in 1855. Its author, Matthew Fontaine Maury, was a lieutenant in the United States Navy.

Lieutenant Maury was to become one of the founders of oceanography. He was a man ahead of his time. He learned to see the oceans as one complex ocean. Although he was a military man, he felt the ocean should bring people together. It should be a place for cooperation, not a source for quarrels.

To a large extent, Maury succeeded in getting people

from many nations to work together in studying the sea. He worked to overcome their suspicions and distrust of one another. The problems he faced were, in many ways, like the problems involved in creating a law of the sea today.

Maury was a bright youngster, but his parents were too poor to send him to a good school. He therefore joined the Navy to get an education. He made many voyages on a man-of-war, sailing around the world several times.

In those days the Navy had no schools. There was no naval academy. Sailors learned from one another, the older, more experienced men teaching the younger. During his time at sea. Maury learned all he knew about navigation from his shipmates. It was enough to make him a good officer and a clever seaman.

But he knew there was much more to learn. In Maury's time navigation was a rough-and-ready craft. Maury talked to many sailors in all parts of the world. He had a knack for getting people to open up and talk about their experiences. He soon found out that the most useful knowledge about navigation was locked in the minds of a small number of the ablest sailors. They had charted the face of the sea in their minds and mapped paths over it. They knew its winds, storms, and currents. They knew where the paths were deep and safe, as well as where sharp reefs lay beneath the shallow waves. These were lessons the mariners had learned from the sea itself.

Maury too was learning from the sea. The sea was his book, and he made up his mind to study every chapter of

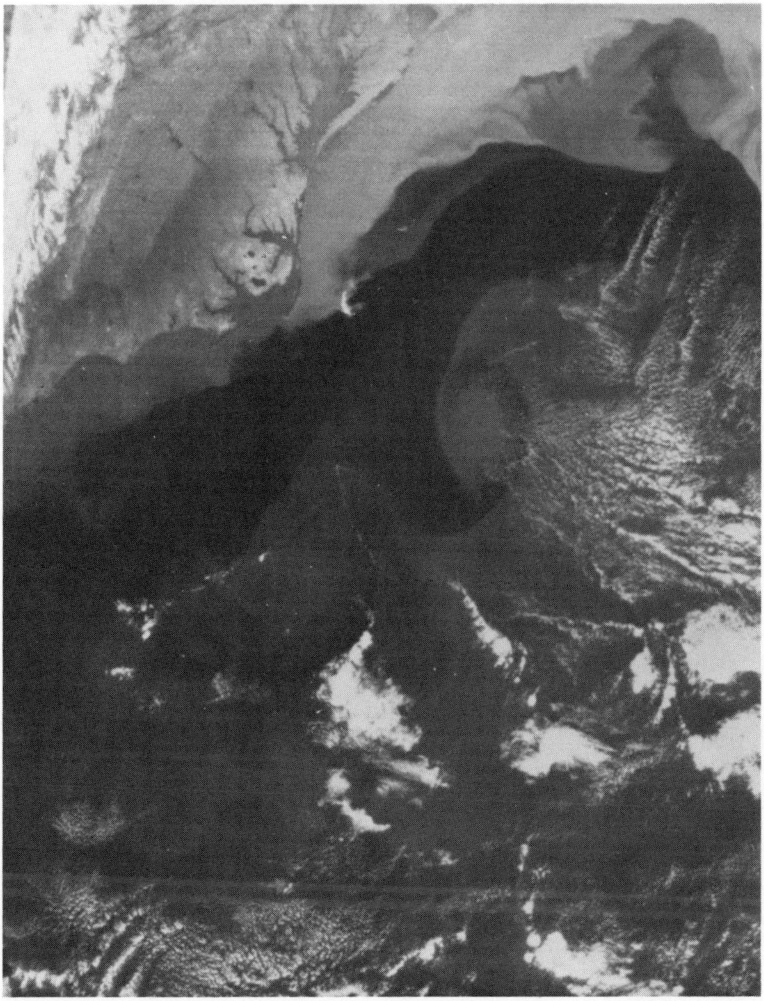

In this photo taken from a space satellite by a camera sensitive to infrared light, the warm waters of the Gulf Stream make it visible as the curve of darker water swirling up the East Coast of the United States. The infrared camera shows the colder waters, the clouds, the land and the snow as gray to white. (NOAA)

it. His goal, he wrote, was "nothing less than to blaze a way through the winds of the sea by which the navigator may find the best path at all seasons."

The sea was too vast a book for any one man to read entirely. He might study much, but he had to rely on what others had found out as well. And others were not so willing to share their knowledge.

A captain of a trading ship knew the tricks of his own routes best—a few lines or a paragraph in the book of the sea. To him, that small store of facts was money. It gave his ship an edge over competitors who did not know the route as well. For each captain the special knowledge of his routes was a carefully guarded business secret.

Maury understood all that, for he was a very practical man. But he saw that all sailors would gain more than they would lose from sharing their knowledge of the ways of the sea. This feeling may have been made stronger by a tragic stagecoach accident in 1839 in which Maury was lamed for life. From that time on, his seagoing career was finished.

After 1839, Maury began collecting data from ships' logs. Other sailors now had to be his reporters. He had to read the sea through their eyes.

In 1842, he became superintendent of the Navy's Depot of Charts and Instruments. All the files of the Navy's old logbooks were now open to him.

It was a confusing picture, like trying to read a book in which the pages had been torn out and put back together in no particular order. What's more, it was a book written by many different hands in different styles. Each captain recorded those things that interested him at times that pleased him.

It had to be put together to be of use. Each mariner, Maury decided, must make regular reports, and they must be pooled: "By putting down on a chart the tracks of many vessels on the same voyage during all seasons, and by [recording] . . . the winds and currents daily encountered, together with latitude and longitude, it was plain that navigators hereafter, by consulting the charts, would have for their guide the results of the combined experience of all ships whose tracks were recorded."

To reach this goal, Maury made up his own blank charts to be used by American mariners everywhere. There were spaces on the charts for twenty-four different kinds of observations—everything from sea and air temperatures and the shapes and appearances of clouds and fog to the kinds of sea life found in the ship's path. Maury also invented a coding system for the records. There were four colors for the four seasons, broken and dotted lines for months, comet tails for wind direction, and arrows for ocean currents.

When the first charts came back, Maury was far from satisfied. There were lots of blank spaces. Some couldn't be helped, for it would take the records of many years and many voyages to cover a small part of the huge area of the oceans. But many of the blank spaces were due simply to carelessness or laziness. The sailors hadn't made all the observations they had been asked to make.

So Maury sent out more charts and more requests. He was good at getting people to cooperate by showing them where their own best interests lay. He pointed out all the blank spaces and the reasons for them. The sailors were told they had to make more of an effort to keep their records more carefully and more accurately. At the end of every voyage, Maury asked that the observations be sent to him at the Naval Observatory in Washington, D.C. In return, the cooperating sailors would get charts pooling the combined knowledge of many ships that had traveled the same route in all seasons of the year. And these charts would be free.

This encouragement worked. "So in a little while," Maury wrote, "there were more than a thousand navigators engaged day and night, and in all parts of the ocean . . . to increase our knowledge as to the winds and currents of the sea, and [as a guide to] its safe navigation and physical geography."

Over the years, more of the blank spaces in the world's oceans were filled in. Maury persuaded hard-headed seamen to work together in the great adventure of coming to a better understanding of the sea. He made them feel the romance of science. One of the many thousands of letters he recieved from shipmasters perhaps sums it up best: ". . . For myself, I am free to confess that for many years I commanded a ship, and although never insensible to the beauties of nature upon the sea or land, I yet feel that until I took up your work, I had been traversing the ocean blindfolded."

Maury gave the seamen practical results, too. In a few years, for example, Maury's charts had cut the travel time from the United States to Australia by twenty days, and to Rio de Janeiro by ten. Even more time was shaved off transatlantic trips. Maury became known as "the pathfinder of the seas."

He was also becoming one of the fathers of oceanography. The knowledge that filled out the charts was rounding out Maury's understanding of the sea. In 1855, he put all of his new-found understanding of the sea and how it

The Norwegian oceanographic ship Fram *frozen in the Arctic ice pack during the 1890s.* (NORWEGIAN INFORMATION SERVICE IN THE UNITED STATES)

works into his *The Physical Geography of the Sea.* In one year, the book went through six printings. Even today, it is a classic on the science of the sea. A new edition was printed in 1963—108 years after the book's first publication.

As we have seen, Maury described the Gulf Stream at the very start of his book. The Gulf Stream is but one of many ocean currents. Maury saw that these currents form a vast system. He called them the arteries of the earth, circulating ocean waters everywhere.

Surface waters are largely driven by prevailing winds. These are winds over certain areas of the globe that blow from the same direction for most of the year. The surface currents are often warm currents, heated by the sun. They flow near the surface because warm water is lighter than cold water.

Cold currents tend to flow along the sea floor. As they near land, the sea floor rises, forcing the cold currents upward. They carry with them rich foodstuffs that have drifted down to the ocean bottom—the remains of the small free-floating plant and animal life living near the surface.

Wherever this happens, these cold currents welling up turn a part of the sea into a pasture for sea life. Off the coasts of Peru and Chile, the upwelling creates the rich anchovy fishing grounds. In the deep ocean the meeting and mixing of cold and warm water currents has a similar effect. At such meeting places are some of the world's most productive fishing grounds.

The ocean and its currents have a powerful effect on

our planet's climate and weather, too. The cold Labrador Current, hugging Canada's east coast, makes it a frigid place in winter. The average winter temperature along the Labrador coast is about 0° F (−18° C). By contrast, the average winter temperature in Edinburgh, Scotland, is 42° F (6° C). Yet Edinburgh is about as far north as parts of the Labrador coast! Narvik, Norway, is 1,000 miles (1,609 kilometers) farther north, beyond the Arctic Circle. But Narvik's average winter temperature is 23° F (−5° C). A major port, Narvik's waters are ice-free all year round! The difference is due to warm water from the Gulf Stream, which flows past both Edinburgh and Narvik.

For 2,000 miles (3,218 kilometers) along the west coast of South America, there is an unbroken stretch of desert, from northern Peru to the Rio Elqui in Chile. There are places in this narrow strip of desert where no rain has fallen in over a hundred years.

A major cause of this desert is the cold Peru Current, the same current that makes the coastal waters teem with fish. Moisture-laden air from the ocean blows toward the desert areas. As it passes over the Peru Current, the air is cooled. It loses its moisture as rain falling over the ocean. By the time the winds reach land, they are bone-dry.

The flow and swirl of ocean currents mixes the ocean waters far and wide. Maury found that seawater samples taken far apart from different oceans were much alike—as if, he wrote, "the two samples had been taken from the same bottle after having been well shaken."

After Maury, the oceans could never seem a simple

highway again. They are one complex world ocean. To Maury, the world ocean itself seemed almost like a living thing.

Even before his book was finished, Maury was writing to scientists all over the world. Having gotten the sailors of his own country to work together, he now called on all seagoing nations to cooperate in exploring the oceans.

In 1853, largely at Maury's urging, the Brussels Maritime Conference met in Belgium. Nineteen countries, all those with large merchant fleets or navies, sat down together to hear a United States Navy lieutenant plead for scientific cooperation among nations on the high seas. At the close of Maury's speech, the delegates stood as one and applauded.

That night Maury wrote to his wife: "Rarely has there been such a sublime spectacle . . . all the nations agreeing to unite and cooperate in carrying out one system of . . . research with regard to the sea. They may be enemies in all else, but here they are to be friends."

After the Brussels conference, the British and American navies worked together on taking depth soundings across the North Atlantic Ocean. These soundings showed how deep the ocean floor was at various points.

The soundings prepared the way for the laying of the first transatlantic cable, which carried telegraph messages between America and Europe. By 1858, the first cable was in place and working, but it did not last long. Two years later it broke.

The broken section was under 6,000 feet (1,829 meters) of water. When it was hauled up for repairs, it was covered with clinging mud from the ocean floor.

It was also covered with deep-sea animals of many different kinds. They were animals that no scientist had ever seen before. The broken cable gave evidence of a whole new world of ocean life in the "lifeless" deeps.

Why lifeless? In Maury's time, most scientists agreed that life in the great ocean depths was impossible for three reasons: darkness, pressure, and cold.

No ray of sunlight penetrates much more than 600 feet (182.9 meters) beneath the surface of the sea. And light gives the energy that the plants of the sea use to make starches and sugar from the simple chemicals in seawater. In much the same way, of course, land plants use sunlight to make starches and sugar from the water in the soil and the carbon dioxide in the air. In the process, both land and ocean plants release oxygen into the air or water.

But below 600 feet (182.9 meters), it was thought these plants could not exist because of lack of light. All other sea creatures either eat these plants or live on creatures that do. So, without the plants, there could be no food in the depths. Nor could there be oxygen, which practically all living things need.

At great depths, the pressure of the seawater is thousands of tons per square inch—more than enough to crush any living thing absolutely flat. And in those depths the temperature always stays around the freezing point. What could possibly live in freezing cold water under enormous pressure and without light or oxygen?

Yet there is life. Living things in the deeps feed on remains drifting down from the sunlit waters above. They prey on one another. Some are luminous, bringing their own light into the sunless deeps. The angler fish dangles a glowing lure over its gaping tooth-filled mouth to attract its victims.

Currents moving downward through the sea bring dissolved oxygen to these creatures. The enormous pressure of the sea on their bodies does not affect them. Their tissues and the inner parts of their bodies are filled mostly with water at the same pressure, so they are in no danger of being crushed.

The broken cable had proved to scientists that many of their ideas about the deep ocean were mistaken. More important, it created great interest in the unknown world at the bottom of the oceans. Part of the interest was practical: How rough is the sea floor? Where can cables be laid safely? What kinds of animals might attach themselves to the cable and perhaps weaken or destroy it? But beyond that there was the challenge of the unknown, which has always fascinated mankind.

In December, 1872, H.M.S. *Challenger* sailed from England to explore the unknown. The *Challenger* was a ship of the British Navy, but for this voyage her guns were removed. She was outfitted with laboratories and winches to haul in and lower her nets. She was the first ship ever whose only purpose was the scientific exploration of the oceans.

Like many ships of her day, the *Challenger* was both a sailing ship and a steam-powered vessel. On her three-and-a-half-year world journey, though, the ship used her sails for traveling. The steam engines were used to hold the ship in position when soundings were being taken or the bottom dredged. The engines also powered the winches.

During her voyage, the *Challenger* stopped at 350 stations, or places on the high seas where the ship remained sometimes for days while scientists studied conditions. They measured the depth of the ocean. They took water temperatures from the top to the bottom of the station. They measured the direction and speed of currents. Animals and plants, most of them never before seen, were taken aboard. So many of them were found that the scientists were crowded out of their laboratories and living quarters. Whenever the *Challenger* came into a new port, animals and plant specimens had to be unloaded and sent back to England to make room for new discoveries.

By journey's end, 4,717 new kinds of plants and animals had been discovered. Parts of the sea floor of every ocean except the Arctic had been explored. The sea floor was found to be uneven. Near the middle of the Atlantic Ocean runs a broad ridge of high underwater mountains. As ocean exploration continued into the twentieth century, much more was discovered about this ridge and others like it.

The sea floor showed other differences from place to place. Here it was covered with mile after mile of the tiny skeletons of one-celled sea plants—skeletons of shapes as different and beautiful as the shifting designs seen in a kaleidoscope. There, the ocean floor was a lifeless carpet of red clay stretching for thousands of miles.

Yet most of the ocean was still unexplored and unknown.

Chapter 4 EXPLORING THE SEA, FROM MAURY TO THE PRESENT

At the 1853 Brussels Maritime Conference, Maury had tried to persuade many nations to work together at sea. He also suggested that they work together on land, too, building a chain of weather-observation stations.

Politely, the same delegates who had cheered his opening remarks refused. To paraphrase Maury's words, on the seas the nations agreed to be friends. On land they agreed to remain enemies or, at best, suspicious rivals.

Why? Although cooperation seemed an easy and simple thing on the oceans, nations had always fought over territory and wealth. That meant land. Land was the major source of wealth. Only in the twentieth century did the sea become a possible source of great wealth. Wars were fought primarily on land and for land. It was true that battles were fought at sea. But they were fought to protect the homeland from invasion or to keep trade routes open to allies and closed to enemies.

The sea was a road without signs. Only the clock, the compass, and the stars showed the mariner his way.

If there was wealth in the sea, it was everyone's—or no one's. The sea floor, except in the shallows near the shores, was beyond man's reach. The fish were there for the taking, in never-failing abundance.

Or so it seemed. But all that was to change.

Our power to exploit the resources of the sea was growing rapidly. Before the end of the nineteenth century, some of the sea's seemingly endless riches were strained to the limit. At the same time, our understanding of the sea was also growing. Both these stories are tied together, and we must follow them together.

Our power to exploit the sea grew with our increasing understanding of the sea. So too, but much more slowly, did the realization grow that there was a need for some kind of international law governing the sea.

To see why that need exists, we must follow the trail blazed by the scientists who explored the sea in all its complexity. We must get some idea of how the sea affects weather, climate, our food supply, and the very survival of life upon this planet.

By the year after the Brussels conference, steam-powered trawlers were starting to replace sail-driven trawlers. The trawl is a cone-shaped net dragged across the sea floor by the motion of the ship. It is more efficient for catching fish than hooks and lines or stationary nets.

Early trawls were held open by a beam. The top of the

trawl's open end was attached to the beam by runners in much the same way that a shower curtain is attached to a rod.

This method was clumsy. Later, floats were used to buoy up the top end of the trawl, and weights to hold down the bottom end. Two kite-shaped doors called otter doors kept the sides of the net apart as it was hauled through the water.

Steam-driven trawlers turned these nets into formidable fishing tools. The steam trawler could travel far and wide without depending on the wind. The power of the steam engine pulled heavy nets along at a good speed like huge mouths agape for fish.

On land, the steam engine was creating more and more demand for fish. As railroad lines spread through Europe and the United States, fresh fish could quickly be carried to many cities and towns. As a result, fishing fleets grew rapidly in size and number.

In 1883, the noted English scientist and writer T. H. Huxley said, "All the great sea fisheries are inexhaustible." Huxley was soon to see his mistake.

By the mid-1880s, something odd was happening. Fishermen had to travel farther and farther to catch the same amount of fish. The old familiar fishing grounds were not yielding the same huge amounts of fish that they once had. This was especially true of the most popular kinds of fish.

What was wrong? To find the answer, careful scientific research was needed. By now, fishing was a big business, and many people were concerned about it. Consequently, there was money available to set up laboratories for marine biology and to pay scientists to staff the laboratories.

Money, of course, was not enough. There had to be scientists interested in the almost brand-new science of marine biology. One of the pioneers was E. W. L. Holt of England. Holt realized that it was useless just to study fish and their habits in tanks in a convenient shoreside laboratory, no matter how big and spacious. The working marine biologist had to get out on the docks and into the trawlers at sea to understand what was happening to the stocks of fish and why.

Holt went to the docks. He sailed the stormy fisheries of the North Sea. And always he asked the same questions: How many fish were breeding in each fishery? How big must a fish—say, a cod or flounder—grow before it is able to breed? How many fish under that size were the trawlers taking?

It was clear that every fish taken under that size would never live to breed new fish. If too many were taken, the next generation of cod or flounder would be smaller in number, and so it would go until there were too few fish of one kind or another left for the trawlers to find. Or perhaps the species might be wiped out altogether.

Holt suggested that fish under breeding size should not be taken. But no one paid much attention. Even now, a century later, there is not much cooperation among nations to manage fishing. On the high seas each country is a law unto itself. It is hard for nations to agree on how to share the food fish of the oceans, and it is even harder for them to agree on what limits it would be wise to place on the fish harvest. Each nation or group of nations suspects others of seeking some advantage at their expense—and often these suspicions are well founded!

Soon other seagoing scientists joined in the search for answers to the problems of fisheries. Why were some areas of the ocean rich in life while others were watery deserts? Why did the number of fish in a place vary so greatly with the season? Why, for example, do the cold waters of the Arctic Ocean and the northern North Atlantic suddenly explode with life in the late spring and early summer? Why are the Grand Banks off Newfoundland and Georges Bank off Cape Cod such rich fishing grounds?

To find the answers to these questions, biologists and other ocean scientists had to trace the chain of life in the sea, for in the sea, as on the land, living things depend on one another in many complex ways.

Among these scientist-explorers was Viktor Hensen, who cruised the North Atlantic in 1889 aboard the S.S. *National.* It was Hensen who coined the word "plankton" to describe the most common kind of life in the sea. The name comes from an ancient Greek word meaning to wander, as does the word "planet." The planets are the wanderers of the sky, as plankton are the wanderers of the ocean. They drift freely and are carried here and there by the winds, the tides, and the currents of the sea. Some, like the jellyfishes and the masses of floating seaweed, are visible to the naked eye.

But by far the greater part of plankton are microscopic plants and animals. Hensen was one of the first to show that all life in the sea—and perhaps on land as well—depends on the invisible one-celled plants that float in uncountable numbers through the sunlit upper layers of the sea. These tiny plants make up the pastures of the sea. Acre after acre, mile after mile, they cover an area far larger than all the dry land of our planet. To try to write down their numbers would, as one scientist has put it, "wear out the zero on a typewriter."

The grasses of our dry-land pastures need roots to anchor them to the ground and to take up water and nourishment from the soil. They need stems to support their leaves, those green sails that spread to catch the light of the sun.

But sea plants need neither stems nor roots nor leaves. They are surrounded by water. The water buoys them up. Dissolved in the water are all the chemicals they need for life and growth. So the more surface sea plants can expose to the water, the better they are able to absorb food. And the smaller the body of an animal or a plant, the larger is its surface area compared with its volume.

For these reasons, all the plants of the high seas are algae. Algae have no true roots, stems, or leaves. Most marine algae are single-cell plants.

Diatoms are among the most important of the marine algae. Each diatom is enclosed in a transparent glassy box. Two shells form the box, one fitting over the other like a lid. The shells are made of silica, the main ingredient of man-made glass. Patterns, often of great beauty, are etched into the shells. The patterns are different for each kind of diatom.

In spring and in fall, the population of diatoms explodes into bloom overnight. Mile after mile of ocean turns golden brown and soupy with a carpet of diatoms. The gold-brown carpet has a metallic shine to it. The shine is due to droplets of oil within each plant cell where food is stored.

Diatoms are commonest in cold waters, but in warmer seas, where their huge numbers sometimes give a reddish color to the water, the fire algae bloom. The Red Sea gets its name from them. Most fire algae are not dangerous to man, but one kind causes the so-called red tide. Poisons produced by this algae are taken up by oysters and other shellfish, and people eating the shellfish become seriously ill and can die.

Fire algae are so named because many of them glow at night. Where they are thickest, every wave and droplet may seem aflame. Oars glow as they dip in and out of the water, and the wake of a ship is traced in rippling lines of light. Along with the diatoms, they are the mainstay of life in the sea.

Where the sea blooms with plant life, it will soon swarm with animals. First come the small animals of the plankton—shrimp, cyclops, the young of crabs, and other creatures. They in turn are eaten by mackerel, herring, and other fish, which are eaten by larger marine animals like tuna and swordfish. And so the food chain goes up to the largest of animals, the great whales and the giant squids. A sperm whale may eat some 15,000 fish in a day. Each of these fish may have eaten some 7,000 smaller creatures in a day. Each of the small plankton feeders may consume 130,000 or so diatoms and other algae in a day.

The remains of the eaten and the dead fall like a steady rain through the deep ocean. They fall from the sunlit surface to the cold, dark sea floor miles below. The glassy shells of uncountable diatoms drift down, as they have for a billion years and more. Over the eons they have carpeted parts of the floor in a rich and beautiful ooze, just as, season by season, the living plants carpet the waves above.

Shown here are a variety of animal plankton. The long eel-like creatures with large heads and eyes (one is just above the letter A) are recently hatched fish. The bulge beneath the eyes is the yolk sac, which holds a supply of stored food for the newborn fish. B are corepods, which are very small and form a large part of the diets of many fish. The ones shown are about .08 of an inch (2 millimeters) long. C and E are fish eggs. D and F show the young of crustaceans such as shrimp and crabs. (NOAA)

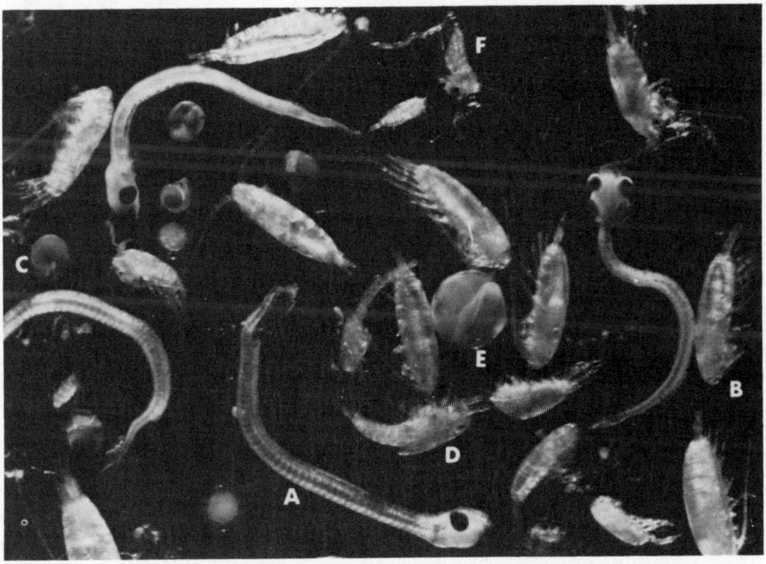

If all this rain of the living stuff of the sea stayed on the ocean floor, the sea would soon be without life. Most of the substances that make life possible would be locked in the depths of the sea. But the ocean is constantly stirred. Winds blow over it. The sun warms the surface waters but not the depths. It warms the waters of the tropics much more than the waters around the poles. Uneven heating and the winds drive the great system of ocean currents, which is one of the forces that makes the sea bloom with life and creates the great ocean fisheries.

The Grand Banks off Newfoundland is an example. Here the eastward-flowing warm water of the Gulf Stream collides with the chill waters of the Labrador Current flowing south. The collision stirs the sea and mixes it to its depths.

Still farther northward flows a long arm of the Gulf Stream, the North Atlantic Drift. It flows more than 1,000 feet (305 meters) beneath the Arctic ice pack.

This warm current beneath the northern ice was discovered in the 1890s by the Norwegian explorer Fridtjof Nansen. Nansen had allowed his ship, the *Fram*, to be frozen into the ice pack so that he could study the Arctic Ocean and trace the movements of the ice. Nansen hoped the drift would carry him to the North Pole.

It did not, but in the months that the *Fram* was adrift in the ice, much was learned about the Arctic. The crew drilled holes through the ice and measured the depth and temperature and saltiness of the water. (Since salt remains crystallized in melting ice, water from the melting Arctic pack is less salty than Atlantic water.)

It was, in fact, the saltiness and warmth of the submarine current that told Nansen what it was—a branch of the Gulf Stream, an offshoot of the Atlantic Ocean running beneath the Arctic.

The nineteenth century ended and the twentieth began. Slowly the oceanographers went on with their work, and slowly the portrait of the oceans grew more intriguing and more complex.

World War I erupted, and the North Atlantic became a battleground. But it was not navy versus navy, with roaring guns and great heroics. It was German submarines versus Allied ships. Only the submariners and the fish heard the hiss and burble of the torpedo streaking from its tube. The explosion came when and if the torpedo found its target. Then it was too late to be a warning.

By 1917, the submarines were taking a heavy toll of Allied shipping. There was a great rush to find ways of detecting the submarines. Their armor and their cloak were the ocean itself. How could they be found in the depths?

The answer was by sound. Water conducts sound far better and over greater distances than does air. Radio waves, on the other hand, do not travel through the sea, and light cannot penetrate the water very far either. But for many centuries man has known the trick of holding a tube to his ear and putting the other end in water to listen for underwater sounds made by faraway ships.

At first, the Allies actually used this method to hunt submerged U-boats. But by war's end, they had developed devices for sending pulses of sound through the water and picking up the echoes. By timing the echo and noting its direction, an enemy submarine could be located.

These devices, developed in war, had more important peacetime uses. They could be used to measure the depth of the sea at any point.

The old methods of taking the depth of the ocean were awkward and none too accurate. Weights were slowly lowered into the sea on lines of rope or wire. Since the average depth of the ocean is 2.3 miles (3.7 kilometers), it took hours to lower the weight to the bottom and more hours to haul it up again.

And how to tell when the weight struck bottom? The line might well go on paying out even after the bottom was reached. The scientists used a rough-and-ready method: they watched for a sudden slowing in the rate at which the line was paying out. When that happened, they considered that the weight had reached the floor of the sea.

That made depth-finding a bit of a guessing game, and other factors made the results even more doubtful. For example, the rope or wire might be bent or twisted or pushed aside by some strong subsurface current. In fact, many of the early measurements of the depth of the oceans were overestimated for this reason.

Echo-sounding was far more accurate because a "beam" of sound could be aimed straight down. Moreover, the sound, traveling at about 4,900 feet (1,494 meters) a second in the sea, would make the round trip in a few seconds at most. So soundings could be made continuously as the ship moved on. This allowed scientists to make a map of the sea floor.

Ironically, the first detailed map of an ocean floor by echo-sounding was a result of war, too. After World War I, Germany was bankrupt. Yet the Allies demanded that Germany pay a staggering amount in war reparations. And it was to be paid in gold. What it all added up to was 50,000 *tons* (45,400 metric tons) of gold. Where was the gold to come from?

Every one of the naturally occurring elements can be found in some form in seawater, and that includes gold. In fact, a single cubic mile of seawater contains some 100,000,000 dollars' worth of gold at 1969 prices. That's probably a lot more at today's prices, whenever you happen to be reading this book.

One hundred million dollars sounds like a lot of money, but the real point is how deceptive figures can be. A cubic mile of seawater is also a lot of water. A cubic mile (6.7 cubic kilometers) of ordinary granite rock contains five hundred times as much gold as a cubic mile of ocean.

Nevertheless, the Germans, in their desperation, sent out the research ship *Meteor* to try to extract gold from the ocean and pay the reparations. In this, the *Meteor* did not succeed.

But in a period of two years, the ship crossed the South Atlantic Ocean a dozen times, making more than 70,000 soundings of the ocean depths. For the first time, scientists had a profile of the floor of an ocean from shore to shore.

The profile revealed some major surprises. The ocean

floor was incredibly rugged and rough—more so than earth's land surface. Around the shores of Europe, Africa, and America lie shallow undersea plains—the continental shelves. They average about 400 feet (122 meters) deep.

Where a shelf ends, often hundreds of miles from the coast, there is a sharp drop. Sheer underwater cliffs plunge straight down to the true sea floor. It is a plunge of miles.

Nor were the ocean deeps between the shelves level plains. They were dotted with seamounts—tall mountains towering up from the sea floor. Their circular tops show them to be the remains of ancient volcanoes.

Running down the center of the Atlantic Ocean is the Mid-oceanic Ridge, an enormous range of undersea mountains. Over the many years since the *Meteor* expedition, scientists have found that this feature of the Atlantic is really only a part of a 40,000-mile (64,400-kilometer) chain of mountains that extends through all the world's oceans. Dividing this worldwide range is a steep rift or valley. In places the rift is up to 30 miles (48.3 kilometers) wide and three miles (4.8 kilometers) deep.

Scientists now think that in ages past all the present continents were joined together in one or two supercontinents. These continents slowly drifted apart, and the great mid-ocean valleys mark the lines of separation.

At some rifts, molten rock is welling up from the hot interior of the earth. These rocks are rich in valuable minerals, especially ores like manganese, copper, nickel, and cobalt. Because the earth is under great strain at the rifts, they are also zones of earthquakes and volcanic activity.

Until recently, no human eyes have ever been able to watch the forces at the rifts in action. In 1979, the small research submarine *Alvin* carried two men down 8,600 feet (2,621 meters) into the East Pacific Rise, a part of the great rift chain. The two scientists watched eruptions of superheated seawater loaded with metal deposits. The eruptions geysered up from vents in the sea floor. Water seeping through the vents came in contact with molten rock and spewed out through the vents again, carrying metal ores from the rocks.

One of the scientists said later that it was like watching the blast furnaces at a steel mill running full tilt. The whole area around the eruptions was blanketed with a crazy-quilt pattern of colored metal ores—yellow, red, ochre, brown, white, and black.

Up to the end of World War II, there were no research submarines, like the *Alvin*, capable of exploring the deep oceans. All submarines were military. After World War II, ocean research went ahead by leaps and bounds, and a number of research subs were built in many countries.

What speeded things up?

A number of things. There were the needs of war and defense, the growing pressures of an expanding human population, and a straining of the food and mineral resources of the land.

After World War II, military submarines became nuclear-powered. That meant they could stay underwater indefinitely, traveling thousands of miles. They didn't even have to come up for air. They could use part of the massive power of their nuclear-powered engines to extract oxygen from seawater.

Hidden in the sea and equipped with missiles carrying H-bomb warheads, a fleet of these submarines is a deadly striking force. Even if an enemy gets in the first blow against the land forces and territory of an opponent, the opponent's submarine fleet will still be there to wreak terrible vengeance. Or so the theory goes.

But to be able to navigate while submerged, never coming up to reveal its presence, a submarine needs far more detailed knowledge of the ocean than existed just after World War II—knowledge of the sea floor, of ocean currents, and much more. To be able to fire its missiles accurately, still more knowledge is needed. For this reason alone, huge sums of money were poured into ocean research.

But as any military officer knows, the development of a weapon calls forth the development of a defense. As we have seen, the only detectors that work effectively undersea are those that use sound. Both the United States and the Soviet Union are building elaborate systems of underwater detectors to keep track of each other's submarines.

The same sophisticated sound systems used for such purposes can also be used for scientific or commercial purposes. They can be used to explore in more detail the sea floor. They can be used to hunt more efficiently for huge schools of fish. They can be used to search for areas of mineral wealth on the sea floor and beneath it. Or they can be used to herd huge "flocks" of fish on giant sea farms.

The sea can supply man's needs for energy, raw materials, and food for ages to come—if it is used wisely. But what is a wise use of the sea? Can each nation pursue its own interests on and beneath the sea without regard for other nations? More than that, can each group of interests within a nation pursue its own use of the sea without regard for other groups? Can all—the energy-producers, the miners, the fishermen, the undersea farmers—seek their own goals without considering the sea as the one great world ocean that it is?

Chapter 5

FISHING THE SEA

It was the time of Cod War III.

Cod War I raged from 1958 to 1961. The second flared up in 1972 and lasted into 1973. The third began in 1976.

The belligerent nations in the cod wars were Iceland and Great Britain. Caught in the middle were the cod.

Cod are not eager swimmers. They will swim fast only when pursuing food or being pursued—and then preferably for only seconds at a time. It may take twelve hours for a cod to recover from a few bouts of vigorous swimming.

The cod in the cod wars had nowhere to go but up—up into the nets and then onto the deck of some fishing boat.

But whose boat was it to be? A part of the British fishing fleet or the Icelandic? That was what the cod wars were about.

They were odd kinds of war. Throughout the hostilities, the Icelanders remained basically friendly toward the English. No shots were fired, but not for lack of guns. Though Iceland has no army, navy, or air force, it does have some small gunboats that make up a coast guard.

The Icelandic Coast Guard boat *Thor* was an early victim of Cod War III. On board the *Thor* for the occasion were some TV cameramen from the British Broadcasting Corporation. They got some dashing shots of two Royal British Navy frigates, *Leander* and *Andromeda*, giving *Thor* what-for. Since *Leander* and *Andromeda* were each three times the size of *Thor* and twice as fast, they ran rings around the Icelandic boat, like mastiffs herding a puppy. They also collided with the *Thor* several times, denting the hull severely and destroying the helicopter deck.

The British Admiralty claimed that the *Thor*'s crew had maneuvered the gunboat into causing the collisions. Unfortunately, the BBC cameras clearly showed the frigates charging and ramming the *Thor*.

All these low jinks on the high seas didn't solve the problem between Iceland and Great Britain in Cod War III any more than they had in the earlier cod wars. And while the cod wars are funny to look back on, the problems that caused them are serious.

As a result of the first two cod wars, Iceland and Great Britain had made a two-year fishing agreement, which allowed Britain to take 130,000 tons (118,000 metric tons) of cod yearly within the 50-mile (80.5-kilometer fishing zone that Iceland had declared around its coasts.

The British wanted to renew the agreement for ten

years. In return, they would accept a lower figure of 110,000 tons (99,860 metric tons) for their yearly catch.

Out of the question, replied Iceland. The most they would offer the British was 65,000 tons (59,000 metric tons), and they were extending their fishing zone to 200 miles (321.8 kilometers).

Why? Because Iceland's marine biologists were warning that cod were being overfished in Icelandic waters. The catch would have to be limited to no more than 230,000 tons (209,000 metric tons) said the scientists. Otherwise, the cod would be wiped out. Nearly half of Iceland's income comes from the sale of cod to other countries.

British scientists put the fishing limits a little higher, but basically they agreed with their Icelandic colleagues. The overfishing, which had reached a high point of 470,000 tons (427,000 metric tons) in 1970, had to stop.

The Icelanders themselves were not without blame in all this. They, along with other nations, have been overfishing the herring in the eastern north Atlantic and around Scandinavia. Some twenty-five years ago, the annual catch of herring in this region was over 1,000,000 tons (910,000 metric tons). Now, even with more efficient fishing methods, the annual catch is less than 10,000 tons (9,100 metric tons)—over a hundred times smaller. This has forced the Icelanders to depend more and more on cod fished in their home waters.

Overfishing in the Atlantic and the North Sea is not

an accident or a result of ignorance. For fifty years, scientists have kept records of catches and the size of the breeding fish populations in these waters. They have known how many fish of a given species could be safely caught each year.

But scientists cannot tell governments or fishing fleets what to do. They can only make suggestions and give warnings, and their warnings are often ignored.

The warnings on the herring were ignored. The Icelanders finally heeded the warnings about the cod when the situation grew desperate. The British were more concerned with the sad state of their own fishing industry. Their politicians knew that accepting Iceland's fishing limits would mean throwing thousands of British fishermen out of work. That could easily be translated into thousands of votes against the government that let it happen.

Britain, in the end, did patch up some sort of compromise with Iceland. The events that forced them to it had nothing to do with science or a sensible conserving of supplies of a valuable food fish, however.

The actions of the Royal Navy in Cod War III might have temporarily reassured some British fishermen. But most of the public grew daily more uncomfortable at the sight of Navy ships shepherding poaching English trawlers in Icelandic waters. Furthermore, the British stand against a 200-mile (321.8-kilometer) zone around home waters was weakened when the United States Senate approved a 200-mile (321.8-kilometer) zone for this country. Then oil was found in offshore drillings in the North Sea. Britain claimed wells, but to do so, it had to adopt its own 200-mile zone.

All countries with large or powerful fleets have behaved in pretty much the same way with respect to their rights and responsibilities in the uses of the sea. As far as fishing goes, the sea is divided up into a number of private ponds. When a pond shows signs of being exhausted, you find another pond. It's just a question of have fleet, will travel.

Since the early 1960s, the North Atlantic Ocean and the North Pacific Ocean have been fished up to their natural limits by the great fishing fleets—those of the European nations, the United States, Korea, Japan, and the Soviet Union. Adding more ships to the fleets in these oceans does not increase the numbers of fish that are caught. All it does is divide the same numbers among more boats, so that each boat's catch is smaller.

So the fleets are moving elsewhere in search of greener pastures. "Greener pastures" is more than just a figure of speech. Off the West African coast, for example, surface currents move away from the land. As a result, the deeper water with its rich supply of nutrients rises to the surface, and the plankton blooms. Here the sea becomes a pasture. Sardines, mackerel, tuna, and other food fish swarm in great numbers.

The best fishing areas are off the coasts of Morocco, Mauritania, and Senegal in North Africa. Here the European, Korean, and Japanese fleets now have many ships. By the end of the 1970s, these fleets were catching more than 70 percent of all the fish caught in these waters.

The fish caught by foreign fleets are not sold in the local markets of the underdeveloped West African states. They are being sold overseas, where the catch commands a high price. The sardine catch, for the most part, does not even go to feed people—at least not directly. The highest prices for sardines are paid by countries like the United States, where the sardines are ground into fish meal to feed livestock.

The West African states do not like having their waters poached by powerful, up-to-date fleets of the developed countries. The fact that a large share of the catch merely goes to fatten livestock makes the poaching even worse from their point of view. Most of the people in these countries live on diets that are poor in protein. Fish, and in particular sardines, would be a cheap and abundant source of protein.

But the fishing "fleets" of these countries consist mainly of canoes and small motorboats, often with primitive nets. They cannot compete with the big fleets. And to modernize their fishing equipment and boats would take large sums of money, which these countries cannot spare.

In an attempt to protect their fishing rights, the West African nations have declared a 200-mile (321.8-kilometer) limit around their coasts. In theory, at least, this means that foreign boats must get permission to fish within 200 miles of the coast. The limit gives the West African states some bargaining power.

One West African nation, Ghana, has tried to build up its own modern fleet to help feed its people. Ghana bought a number of freezer-trawlers from several European countries in the 1960s. These are trawlers with refrigerated compartments to keep the catch until it is ready to be used. The Ghanians also hired European crews to run their ships while local people were being trained to take over.

The scheme failed. Ghana ran out of money to keep the fleet going. Ironically, the reason that Ghana ran out of money was that it was trying to feed its own people! Had the Ghanians sold the bulk of their catch to the highest bidder on the world market, they would have had ample funds to keep the fleet going. But that of course would have defeated the very purpose for which the fleet was intended.

Meanwhile, science and technology are making the big fishing fleets ever more efficient. As we have seen, radio waves do not travel any distance in the sea. But sound travels enormous distances. Almost all marine animals make a large variety of underwater sounds—from the clicking of shrimp to the complex language-like signals of dolphins, porpoises, and whales. And many sea animals are sensitive to even very weak electrical fields in the sea. This sensitivity may help them migrate long distances across the ocean and find their way back to their starting point again.

Sound and electricity are now being put to use to catch fish. The sounds of the fish eating bait are tape-recorded. These sounds are amplified and played back through hydrophones—underwater loudspeakers—bringing the fish to the boat in swarms. United States boats use electricity to concentrate and draw menhaden (a herringlike fish) toward one end of the huge net in which the fish are caught. There the fish are drawn directly up into the hold of the ship by a suction pump.

Sounding gear and satellite photos are used to keep track of large schools of fish. In the near future, automated buoys at many places in the world's oceans will signal the presence of food fish to central computers, and the fleets will move out to take immediate advantage.

Even today, the Russian fishing expeditions are planned with great precision. Once a rich fishing area is found by careful research, a whole armada of ships is sent out. There are large and small trawlers and huge factory ships which process almost everything that is caught. The higher-quality fish are canned and frozen right on board the factory ship. Poorer-quality fish are processed into meal and oil.

Many of these poorer-quality fish are not used by United States fishermen because they would not sell in the American market. This is really more a matter of habit, of what people are accustomed to eating, than anything else.

But the Russian system of finding food in the sea seems thorough and efficient only in comparison with the American system. In actual fact, the ways in which man exploits the sea for food make very little sense in terms of his own self-interest. There are millions of species of plants and animals in the sea. Many are edible or might be made edible. But 90 percent of all the food taken from the sea is fish.

estimate of 1.3 billion tons (1.2 billion metric tons) may not be too accurate.

Scientists would like to get a reasonably accurate estimate of the number of Antarctic krill *before* large-scale krill fishing beings. That way, they may be able to set a sensible limit before the free-for-all of competition for krill increases the danger of overfishing.

This may be very important for man because krill, used wisely, could be a large part of the solution to the world's food problems.

Equally important, krill is the cornerstone of life in the Antarctic. Whales, seals, birds, and fish feed on krill. And the remains of dead krill, carried by north-flowing cold currents from the Antarctic, may spread nutrients throughout the oceans of the world.

No one knows for sure the complex role that krill may play in the life of the oceans. It may take many years to unravel the whole story—if indeed anything so complex can ever be taken apart completely.

Krill must and should be used as food. But it would seem wise to be cautious in that use and not to endanger the basic supply of krill. Once endangered, we may start a trend that cannot be reversed. To cause damage that cannot be mended, when we have no idea how far the effects of that damage might spread, does not seem sane.

Chapter 6 DOWN IN THE FARM

Sunday, May 8, 1994:

A week of this work now. I'm really beginning to enjoy it. The strangeness is fun.

On calm days, the sky is like a mirror a few feet over my head. When I look up, I can see myself and a part of the farm reflected in it. But when a breeze starts blowing, my sky ripples. All the reflections break into bits and pieces, dancing and shaking.

Soon everything begins to dance. Row after row, the leaflike fronds of Porphyra *wave in the blue-tinged sunlight as if keeping time with the ripples gliding across the sky. I float among them, rocking to the same rhythm. It's hypnotic. The wind rocks the sea and the sea rocks me. . . .*

The diarist is not on another planet. She is a diving farmer down in a farm off the west coast of the United States. The reflecting "sky" that wrinkles in a breeze is the surface of the ocean. Even a short distance beneath the waves, the water begins to filter out a part of the yellow and red from sunlight, making it look a little more bluish.

What does she grow in her farm? Seaweed and microscopic algae that serve as food for oysters. Wastes produced by the oysters in turn help feed the seaweed. Abalone, another kind of shellfish, feed on the seaweed.

The ocean pasture patrolled by our sea farmer of the future is blooming with microscopic algae. We saw in Chapter Four that parts of the sea bloom in spring and fall when upwelling currents bring nutrients to the surface. But the bloom of the sea farm does not depend on the seasons. It lasts all year around.

The nutrients on which the algae grow come not from the ocean floor but from the land. Water from a nearby sewage treatment plant flows through the farm. In the sewage plant, solids have been filtered out. Harmful bacteria have been killed. Toxic chemicals have been removed. The remaining dissolved wastes are rich in phosphates, nitrates, and other chemicals needed for rapid growth of the algae.

In fact, the sea farm is actually the last stage in a highly efficient sewage system—a system in which very little is wasted. The human and animal wastes from the land are fertilizers for the sea farm. Those wastes are used up by the animals and plants of the farm in feeding and growing. The products of the farm are returned to the land as food and a number of other useful materials.

For example, let's take *Porphyra*. It is a common seaweed that grows around the world from the Arctic Ocean to the southernmost coasts of South America, Africa, and Australia. *Porphyra*, whose common name is laver, grows on rocks and dock pilings from the low-tide to the mid-tide zones, and much is harvested from the rocks off the coasts of California.

Laver is rich in proteins and vitamins, especially C and B_2. It is used as a food in many countries. In South Wales the fronds are baked into laver bread. The dried leaves are boiled and eaten with lemon juice, spices, and butter.

In Japan, laver is called *nori*. It is a special delicacy, used to wrap and give flavor to other foods such as fish and shrimp.

The Japanese grow large amounts of nori on sea farms around their coasts. Farming the sea is a multimillion-dollar business in Japan. The Japanese farm a variety of sea life, including oysters and other shellfish and shrimp.

The nori is grown on strips of plastic netting to which the seaweed can cling. The strips are about five feet (1.5 meters) wide and 150 feet (45.7 meters) long. The netting, hung from poles, is stretched horizontally a short distance below the surface of the sea. It looks something like huge seaweed-covered ribbons. Each ribbon may hold up to 3,000 fronds, and the fronds can be picked several times during each growing season. (Like many land plants grown for food, laver is an annual.)

A number of other seaweeds are commonly used as food. The most well known are henware, fan kelp, and dulse. At present, not much seaweed is eaten by people in the United States. Like the avoidance of poorer-quality fish, this is largely a matter of taste and custom. Although it is true that some parts of the seaweeds' tissues are not digestible, they are a fair source of protein and a good source of vitamins and important minerals such as iodine.

Fan kelp, along with vine kelp, is widely harvested in the United States as a source of alginic acid, a jellylike substance used as a stabilizer or thickener in ice cream, syrups, puddings, salad dressings, toothpastes, lotions, photographic film, and paints. Alginic acid and the alginates derived from it are nontoxic and partly digestible, which makes them ideal as food additives. Fan kelp is also used by the ton in Russia and Japan as a fertilizer on land-based farms.

Another jellylike material derived from seaweed is carrageen, from Irish moss. It has much the same uses as the alginates and in addition is used in making cosmetics, shaving soaps, shoe polish, and blancmange (a pudding), in curing leather, and in sizing (stiffening) cloth. Starch is a common sizing used with cloth. But the sizings made from seaweed are more easily soluble in water and form a tougher, more elastic film in the cloth. The manufacture of carrageen from Irish moss is a large industry centered at Scituate, Massachusetts.

Still another useful seaweed product is agar. Dissolved in hot water, agar sets to a firm jelly. Unlike jellies made from gelatin, seaweed jellies do not soften in hot weather. So agar is used by bakeries to keep cake icings from getting sticky in the summer months. For the same reason, it is used in jellied candies, marshmallows, and candy bars. Even more important, agar is used in medical and bacteriological laboratories. It is a main ingredient in the

Japanese sea farmers harvesting oysters.
(JAPAN INFORMATION CENTER,
CONSULATE GENERAL OF JAPAN)

jellies used to grow colonies of bacteria for various tests. Much of the agar used in the United States is produced near Beaufort, North Carolina, from the seaweed Ceylon moss.

Last, and not least, seaweeds can be decorative. Gulfweed is so named because if floats in large masses in the Gulf Stream. The Japanese use the dried plants of a seaweed closely related to gulfweed for decorating rooms on New Year's Day, much as holly is used for a Christmas decoration in Western countries.

Though our imaginary sea farm is placed in the future, farming the sea is very old. In fact, most of the ideas that are now used in sea farming began long ago with fresh-water farming in ponds.

Fresh-water farming in China started about 1000 B.C. The early ponds were stocked with one kind of fish, a carp. Starting with 20 carp about to bear young, a pond could yield some 240,000 fish, each weighing around three pounds (1.4 kilograms). All that was needed was care and a couple of years.

By 600 A.D., the Chinese pond farms had become whole systems. Six kinds of carp were grown in each pond. One, the grass carp, fed on the surface carpet of aquatic plants. Two other species fed in the deeper waters: one on the plant plankton, the other on the animal plankton. Three species of carp were bottom dwellers and feeders. They fed on mollusks, worms, and the wastes of the grass carp.

Such pond farms are still in use in China. The idea, nearly two thousand years old, is a model for our imagined sea farm of the future. It was, and is, a method of farming in which very little is wasted.

From the Middle Ages to the present, the methods of fresh-water farming have been put to use on salt-water farms throughout Southeast Asia. Salt-water ponds are created in coastal wetlands. These are areas of low-lying coasts where swamps are periodically flooded by the incoming ocean tides.

The swamps are cleared and diked with embankments of mud to make two kinds of ponds. One is the nursery pond. This is stocked with the fry of various salt-water fishes, usually milkfish and mullet.

Fry are freshly hatched young of fish. Almost microscopic in size, they feed on microscopic plankton in the nursery ponds. The nursery ponds must be stocked from the open sea because until recently it was impossible to get the fish to breed in captivity.

While the fry are feeding and growing in the nursery pond, the production ponds are being made ready for them. Like the fresh-water carp ponds, these production ponds have a self-sustaining community of salt-water life—algae, worms, and other plankton.

As soon as the fry are big enough to feed successfully on this larger plankton, they are transferred to production ponds. In a few months to a year, the fish are full-sized and ready to be eaten. Every few months, a well-tended pond of this kind will produce about 500 pounds (226.8 kilograms) of fish for each acre.

Long before anything was known about the seasonal blooms of algae on the open sea—a bloom created by mineral-rich bottom water surging to the surface—sea farmers discovered the need for mixing the waters in their ponds. The best way to do this is to make two sluice gates in the dams that separate the pond from the sea. One gate at the top allows the surface water to flow out to sea as the algae exhaust the nutrients from it. Another sluice at the bottom of the dam allows the nutrient-rich deeper water to flow in from the sea.

Down in our imaginary farm, this was taken care of by a flow of water from the sewage plant. Is this practical? Will it work?

It has been done on a small scale at the Woods Hole Oceanographic Institution in Massachusetts. There, marine scientist John Ryther operates a sea farm much like the one described at the beginning of this chapter. In addition to the microscopic algae, seaweeds, oysters, and abalone, sandworms at the bottom of the tank feed on the wastes from the oysters. The sandworms are in turn eaten by flounder. The whole system is supplied with sewage from a nearby plant.

Ryther says that a 50-acre (20.2-hectare) farm like this, using the treated sewage from a town of 11,000 people, would produce 1,000,000 pounds (453,600 kilograms) of edible shellfish meat a year. He points out that there are about one billion acres (405,700,000 hectares) of coastal wetlands in the world.

Suppose that just one-tenth of these lands were put aside for aquaculture—sea farming. That would amount to 100,000,000 acres (40,570,000 hectares). "The potential yield," Ryther writes, "using improved methods

In 1974, an electric power plant on the Delaware River in New Jersey started using waste heat for aquaculture. The photo shows rainbow trout being harvested in the spring after growing all winter in raceways containing the heated water from the plant's cooling system. In the river the trout would have stopped growing during the winter months when the temperature fell below 40° F (4° C). Since 1974 the power company has sold about 6,000 trout a year to New Jersey for restocking state fishing ponds. Scientists hope this experiment in aquaculture will become a model for many future projects. (PUBLIC SERVICE ELECTRIC AND GAS COMPANY, NEWARK, NEW JERSEY)

of production, would be 100 million tons of food a year —the equivalent of the potential yield from the world's commercial fisheries."

One problem with fish farms has been the difficulty of getting the fish to breed in captivity. The International Developmental Research Centre (IDRC), which is a publicly owned corporation set up by the Canadian government to adapt science and technology to the needs of developing countries, is financing a lot of research in aquaculture. One such project has found a way of getting milkfish and carp to breed in captivity.

The fish are injected with hormones from the pituitary glands of Pacific salmon that are being processed for canning. Hormones are kinds of chemical messengers produced by certain glands. They help control the behavior and development of animals at different times in their lives. The salmon were caught as they were returning to the rivers and getting ready to breed after years of ocean life. This change in their behavior is produced in large part by hormones. So the researchers assumed that these hormones might also influence the captive fish on the farms to breed. And it seems to be working.

Equally promising is IDRC research on increasing the numbers of oysters and mussels produced in aquaculture. Oysters and mussels do not move around, so they do not need to be fenced in. They feed on microscopic plants and animals. Large numbers of them can be crowded into a relatively small space and still remain healthy. They are an excellent food source. For all these reasons, they are ideal animals for aquaculture.

In experiments off the coast of Singapore, IDRC has raised 551 pounds (250 kilograms) of mussels per 10.76 square feet (1 square meter). This points to a yield of about 40.5 tons (36.8 metric tons) of protein from one acre of sea farm. By contrast, an acre of farmland will yield about a half a ton of high protein soybean.

Ryther envisions 100,000,000 tons (97,800,000 metric tons) of high protein food from 100,000,000 acres (40,570,000 hectares) of wetlands, or about a ton an acre. The IDRC research suggests a yield even higher than that—in fact, over forty times higher.

By contrast, the amount of fish being *caught* each year is going down. From 1970 to 1975, the number of large fishing vessels—those over 100 tons (90.8 metric tons)—in the world's fleets went up by 50 percent. But the total catch did not go up at all. So what was happening was that the same amount of fish was being divided up among more and more ships that were more and more costly to build. The result is simple economics. Fish gets more expensive.

Now, as was mentioned in the last chapter, the numbers of fish caught are actually declining. That result is simple to predict, too, but it has nothing to do with economics. Fish are being overfished. Their numbers are going down. It doesn't matter how many dollars in profit are earned by country X or company Y from selling high-priced fish. X and Y could toss all their money right back into the sea, and it would not produce one single extra fish. Nor, of course, can the money be eaten. It can be used to buy food, but only as long as there is food around to be bought. Perhaps the limits of nature should be a part of economics, too.

That brings us back to the situation on land. Once upon a time, people thought there was no limit to how much food could be grown on the land. They knew that the amount of land was limited, but the miracles of technology seemed unlimited. Use more fertilizer per acre. Breed crops that produce more food per acre. Create a "green revolution."

It worked spectacularly for a while. As late as 1950, each extra ton of fertilizer produced a 10-ton (9.1-metric-ton) increase in the world grain harvest.

And then it didn't work so well. The yield per extra ton began to go down steadily. It is still going down, now about half what it was in 1950. The increase in food production from the land is not keeping pace with the increase in the world's population.

Why? For one thing, the good land is already in use. Even the half-good land is in use. Farmers are trying to squeeze extra production from land that is too dry or too stony or too sandy. As for using still more fetilizer, there's a catch there, too. Aside from the problem of poisoning the land with too much fertilizer, the synthetic fertilizers are getting more and more expensive. Many are made from oil, and one thing is certain—oil is scarce and expensive, and it will be a little scarcer and a little more expensive with each tick of the clock.

Is aquaculture going to solve our food problems? Will kids growing up today farm in the sea? Maybe. But it is not likely to happen so soon and so easily. This may seem odd since there is a great variety of sea farms in existence today. Yet all of these farms are in coastal waters, not very far out to sea. This is true despite the fact that coastal sea farming has serious problems. Because the farms are in shallow water, a low tide may leave the animals and plants with dangerously little water. And the fast-moving ebb and flow of the tides makes it hard to add fertilizer or food to the farm. Most is washed out to open sea by the swift currents.

Why, then, do the farms hug the coastlines? The answers to that question sum up the problems now in the way of building larger and more complex sea farms.

Building and running a sea farm is expensive. A lot of money has to be put into the project before it will begin to pay for itself. Few people have enough money of their own to turn a sea farm into a profit-making business.

The money must be borrowed, usually from a bank, but no bank would be willing to lend money for a sea farm outside of coastal waters. According to international law, no person, company, or nation could establish ownership of such a farm.

Even farms within coastal waters are affected by this idea of freedom of the seas. The "soil" of a sea farm is a part of the ocean's waters. It is always in motion. The soil of a land farm stays in one place; the soil of a sea farm eventually travels around the world. A sea farm may be affected by events hundreds or even thousands of miles away. An oil slick from a supertanker spill or an uncapped oil well on the ocean floor can destroy a sea farm.

Oysters and other shellfish are able to concentrate

chemicals from seawater in their bodies. The concentrations may be hundreds or thousands of times greater than in the seawater itself. When poisonous substances such as mercury are dumped into the sea, they are greatly diluted by the huge mass of water. But shellfish growing hundreds of miles from the source of pollution can build up the poisonous chemicals to dangerous strength. From 1956 to 1970, untold thousands of Japanese were poisoned by eating fish contaminated with mercury from wastes dumped into the sea by a chemical factory. Though the poisoning began around Minimata, the city where the factory was located, it gradually spread around Japan. The sickness became known as the Minimata disease, and its effects have cropped up since in many parts of the world.

It may be possible to set aside some parts of the sea for farming, some for fishing, some for mining, and some for drilling for oil and gas, and so on. But it will take careful research and preparation to make sure that one kind of use of the sea does not interfere with a different use of another part of the sea. And that will take a lot of cooperation. It will take cooperation among many different kinds of scientists—physicists, chemists, and biologists, for example. It will take cooperation among many different nations. It will take cooperation among many different business interests, as well.

Chapter 7 THE TREASURES OF THE SEA

The sea is the oldest—and the newest—source of mineral wealth. Since the days of the cave dwellers, people have gotten at least one important mineral from the sea—salt. As far back as 2200 B.C., Chinese writings describe how to get salt from seawater, using the sun's heat to evaporate the water. Today the same methods are still in use wherever salt is extracted from the sea.

Although we could not live without some salt in our diets, it is such a common seasoning that it seems unimportant nowadays. Yet in ancient times, salt was a luxury. Wars were fought over it. The reminder that salt was once a treasure is part of our language. *Sal* is the Latin word for salt. *Salarium*, in the days of ancient Rome, was the money paid to soldiers so they could buy their supply of salt. Later, the word came to mean pay or wages. And it has passed into English as "salary." Other reminders of salt's ancient value are phrases like "worth his salt" and "salt of the earth."

The sea is a dilute broth of many chemicals besides common salt. When seawater is evaporated, all these chemicals are left behind. From them, two other minerals are extracted—magnesium and bromine.

Magnesium is a light metal often used with aluminum in making airplane parts. About 95 percent of the United States supply of magnesium is extracted from seawater at the Dow Chemical plant in Freeport, Texas.

Bromine is a chemical element in the same family as iodine and chlorine. It is a dark-red fuming liquid with a choking and irritating smell. It is used as a disinfectant and in the manufacture of antiknock compounds for gasoline. Knocking happens when gasoline burns unevenly in the engine of a car. This wastes fuel, puts an extra strain on the engine, and makes it turn noisily with a banging or knocking sound. About 80 percent of the United States' supply of bromine comes from seawater.

There is plenty of iodine in seawater also, but it is hard to extract. So we let seaweeds do the chemical work for us. Seaweeds, especially the various kinds of kelp, are rich in iodine. Pure iodine is a solid made up of blackish-gray crystals. The crystals dissolve easily in alcohol, forming a purple solution called tincture of iodine, which is used as an antiseptic.

A small amount of iodine in the diet is required for good health. Iodine is needed for the proper working of the thyroid gland in man and other animals. Processed seaweeds are fed directly to cattle and other farm animals as a source of iodine. Iodine derived from seaweed is also used as a food supplement in human diets.

But the real mineral wealth of the sea is not dissolved in its waters. It lies spread across the floor of the sea and buried beneath that floor.

It was the scientists aboard H.M.S. *Challenger*, returning to England in 1876, who brought back the first hint of this great wealth. As we have seen in Chapter Three, the *Challenger* left England in December of 1872 to explore the world's oceans. Day after day, the steam-driven winches of the *Challenger* hauled dredges up from the deep sea floor a mile or more beneath the ship. Along with the ooze and the clay and the fascinating variety of new plants and animals, the dredges brought up heavy potato-shaped rocks. For the most part, they were golf-ball to grapefruit-sized. Jet black at first, they turned to a brown and earthy color as they dried.

What are they? Scientists are still studying them today. Sliced through, their centers reveal a structure more like that of an onion than a potato. The rocks are made up of layer upon layer of thin shells of metal ore. Layers of manganese oxide alternate with layers of iron hydroxide and ores of other metals, especially nickel, copper, and cobalt. Manganese makes up the bulk of the rocks. They are about 25 to 30 percent manganese. About 5 percent is cobalt, one to 1.5 percent is nickel, 1 percent is copper, and there are traces of twenty-five other metals. Because they all contain fairly large amounts of manganese, they were given the name manganese nodules.

A raindrop needs a microscopic crystal or a speck of dirt around which to form. So it is with these metal-rich rocks. At the heart of each is some bit of litter that had sunk to the bottom in ages past—a shark's tooth, the ear bone of a whale, a spongy mass of volcanic ash, a bit of rock carried by an iceberg from a polar sea.

The amounts of copper, nickel, cobalt, and manganese in the nodules might make them worthwhile for deep-sea mining of these metals. On land, copper, for example, is mined from ores that contain as little as .7 percent of the metal. But the men of the *Challenger* had no idea how scarce or plentiful the nodules might be.

At the turn of the century, the American naturalist Alexander Agassiz discovered that large quantities of nodules lay on the sea bed of the South Pacific Ocean off South America. His ship, the *Albatross*, hauled up plenty of nodules from every site that he dredged. The sites he explored covered an area as large as the United States.

It was not until after World War II, however, that scientists and mining engineers were actually able to *see* this mineral wealth spread out before their eyes. It was about 1950 when the first deep-sea cameras were invented.

Such a camera is pressure-proof, built to withstand the weight of tons of water miles down in the ocean. It is lowered on a thin, strong steel wire to the ocean floor. An electronic flash unit is suspended from the same wire since no sunlight at all reaches the depths of the sea. Both camera and flash unit are aimed downward at an angle toward the sea floor. The camera and flash can be triggered when a weight hanging beneath them touches the sea floor. Or the correct distance from the floor for a picture can be measured by a sound-ranging device.

Photographs taken with such cameras showed manganese nodules strewn over the sea floor for mile after mile. There are trillions of tons of nodules in the oceans. The Pacific Ocean alone holds an estimated 1.5 trillion tons (1.36 trillion metric tons).

How do they form? The full story is not yet known. Every bit of hard rock surface on the deep sea floor, every piece of clay or fragment of bone or stone, is slowly "painted" with layers of these metallic ores.

"Slowly" is the right word. The ores are laid down in thin layers, almost atom by atom. The nodules grow at the rate of about .08 to .16 of an inch (2 to 4 millimeters) per million years.

But a million years is a short time compared with the age of the earth. Nodules have formed around the teeth of sharks that have been extinct for 25,000,000 years. Nodules weighing several pounds are common. Some are too big for any dredge. In 1955, a British cable-laying ship brought up a one-ton (.9-metric-ton) nodule from 18,000 feet (5,486 meters) down off the Philippines. The nodule was tangled in a snarl of old telegraph cables.

The metallic ores that form the nodules are in solution in the seawater. They may have been dissolved as the water percolated through molten rocks in rifts on the sea floor—an event witnessed by scientists aboard the *Alvin*, as we described in Chapter Four. Or the ores may have come into the sea from other sources.

The nodules do not form where undersea currents are strong enough to scour away any deposit as fast as it is laid down. Nor do they form where the seas are rich in life. There the tiny skeletons of diatoms and the hard parts of other once-living things drift to the bottom in a steady, gentle rain. Anything larger than a grain of sand is quickly covered by this rain of particles.

The richest deposits are deep in mid-ocean in a band about 125 miles (201.1 kilometers) across. The band lies east-west along the southern edge of the equatorial belt in the Pacific, Atlantic, and Indian oceans.

The copper, cobalt, nickel, and manganese they contain are vital to modern technology. Of the four, only copper is available in any quantity from United States-

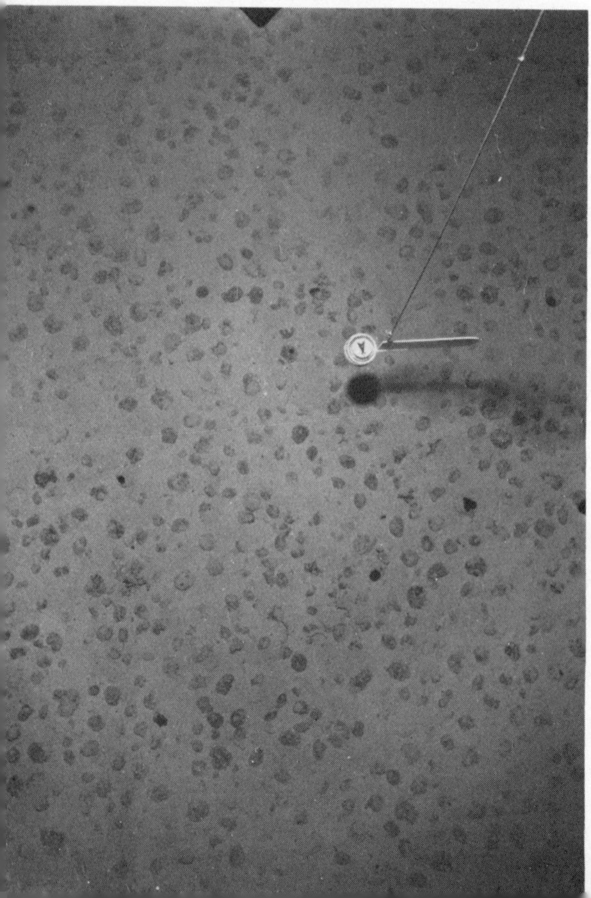

Manganese nodules photographed with a deep-sea camera at a depth of approximately 3 miles (5,000 meters) in the Equatorial Pacific Belt from the NOAA ship Oceanographer. (NOAA)

owned mines. The United States depends almost completely on imports for the other three metals.

These metals are also in short supply in most of the highly industrialized countries. But mining them from nodules miles down on the sea floor—however plentiful the nodules may be—is an enormous engineering job. It's been compared to standing on top of a skyscraper at night and trying to suck pebbles up through a straw from the street.

In fact, one mining method that's being tried out fits that description quite well. It uses a dredge that is hauled along the ocean bottom like the mouth of a gigantic vacuum cleaner.

Traveling at two to three knots and guided by an underwater television camera, the dredge forces the nodules into a large-diameter pipe made of several flexible segments. The pipe feeds into the hold of the mining vessel at its top. Compressed air, pumped down from the ship, forces the nodules upward through the pipe.

This kind of mining needs too much of an investment in money and time for one company to tackle. So it's being undertaken by consortiums—groups of companies pooling their money and know-how for a common purpose.

For example, there is Ocean Mining Associates, which is a partnership of U.S. Steel, the Sun Oil Company, Union Minière of Belgium, and Samin of Italy. There is Ocean Management Inc. (OMI), which is made up of a consortium of British and German companies. OMI is not to be confused with Ocean Minerals Company, which consists of the Lockheed Corporation, Standard Oil of Indiana, Royal Bos Kalis of the Netherlands, and Royal Dutch/Shell. There is Afternod, a French consortium, and also the Kennecott Consortium, which involves companies in many countries, among them the United States, Japan, Great Britain, and Spain.

In the summer of 1978, OMI, using the vacuum-cleaner method, hauled up some 1,100 tons (1,000 metric tons) of nodules about 990 miles (1,600 kilometers) southeast of Hawaii. This was the first successful attempt at mining manganese nodules on a large scale.

The next spring, the research sub *Alvin* discovered the metal deposits along the rift of the East Pacific Rise, where the ores may extend for 1,000 miles (1,609 kilometers) or so. This and other rift systems in the oceans may be another source of mineral wealth.

Yet the companies that have put hundreds of millions of dollars into setting up sea-mining operations are moving ahead very cautiously. And they are keeping whatever technological shortcuts and problems they've discovered close secrets.

Why? Because there are many unanswered questions about mining in the deep sea. Who owns these resources? Who can profit from mining them? How can the profits and the use of the resources be shared?

The United Nations and the various governments that make up that organization have been struggling to find answers to these questions for more than ten years. Now technology is moving ahead faster than the laws and rules that control it. At the same time, companies are reluctant to put a lot of money into a project like deep-sea mining when they fear there is a chance the whole operation may be taken over by some international agency. Should that happen, the companies might find that all of the money they invested has been lost.

Oil is another source of mineral wealth beneath the sea. Usable undersea oil deposits are generally found on the continental shelves and the continental margins, not in the deep sea.

Such shelves surround the shores of all continents. They are shallow undersea plains, averaging about 400 feet (122 meters) deep. The shelves vary greatly in width. Off the coasts of the Mediterranean Sea, for example, the shelf is almost nonexistent. Off the northeastern United States, the shelf is about 100 miles (160.9 kilometers) wide. Off Siberia it is 150 miles (241.4 kilometers) wide.

The continental shelves slope gently down from the shoreline to their outer edge. At the margin, between the shelf and the true ocean floor, the slope becomes steeper.

The continental shelves are generally recognized as making up part of the "economic zone" of the nations on which the shelves border. So the drillers for undersea oil have not run into the legal problems of ownership that the mineral miners worry about. The sites where companies have struck oil off the shores of California and in the Gulf of Mexico were leased from the United States government or from the government of Mexico. The United States is also leasing drilling sites in the Georges Bank off the eastern United States, one of the richest fishing areas in the world. Three-fourths of all the fish caught off the east coast, from Nova Scotia to South Carolina, are caught in the Georges Bank.

Fishermen and environmentalists fought hard against leasing the Georges Bank seabed—more than 660,000 acres (267,000 hectares) of it—to oil and gas developers. Even Richard A. Frank, Administrator of the National Oceanic and Atmospheric Administration, which agreed to the leasing, admitted there was a problem. He said, "The risks of oil drilling on Georges Bank should not be underestimated; they are serious."

Georges Bank is a submarine plateau 50 to 200 miles (80.5 to 321.8 kilometers) off Cape Cod, Massachusetts. About 10,000 years ago, the bank was a tree-covered island. Though the island is now submerged, the depth of the sea in Georges Bank is very shallow—usually less than 300 feet (91.4 meters).

The bank lies between the southward-moving cold Labrador Current and the northeast-flowing Gulf Stream. The water on the plateau turns slowly in a clockwise direction. This "big ball of water," as one scientist describes it, is one of the many unsolved puzzles of the sea. Oceanographers have found that similar swirls of water form on both sides of the Gulf Stream. On the north side, these Gulf Stream rings swirl clockwise and have a core of warm water. On the south side, they swirl counterclockwise and a have a cold core.

The rings form when a loop or bend in the Gulf Stream flow closes up and pinches off from the current. A ring may last as long as three years—a separate, distinct

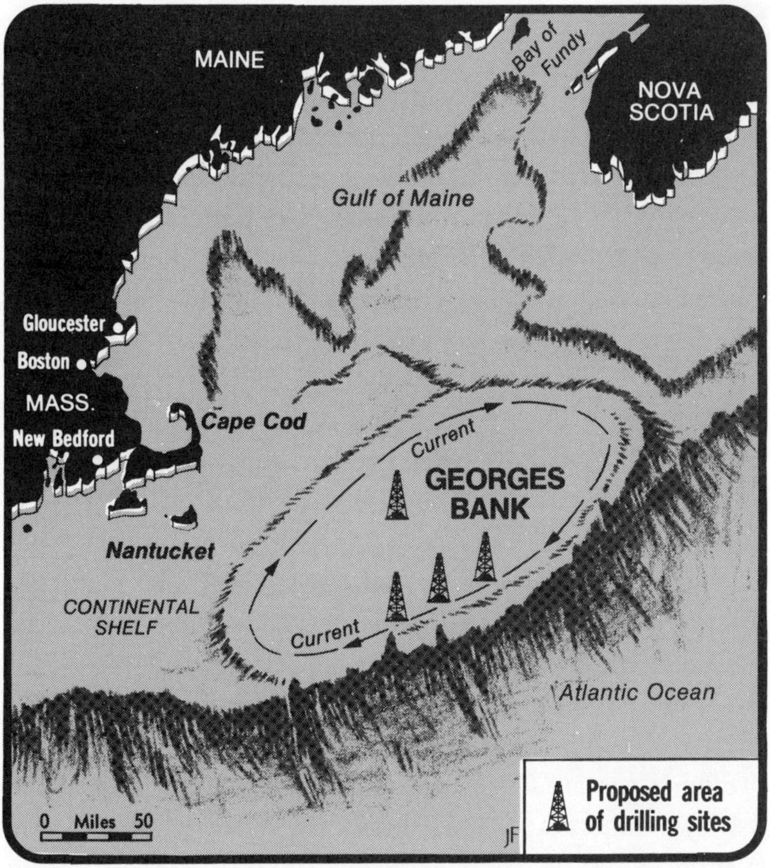

The slow swirl of currents around the Georges Bank keeps food and dissolved oxygen circulating. As a result, the bank is an important spawning ground for many kinds of food fish. If there is a spill from proposed oil drilling in the area, the toxic oil will be spread by the same currents, and damage to the Georges Bank may be severe. (JOAN FORBES IN THE CHRISTIAN SCIENCE MONITOR © 1979 TCSPS)

"piece" of water in the midst of the ocean. Then it may break up or rejoin the Gulf Stream.

Practically nothing is known of why rings last so long and why they finally disappear. Only in the 1970s did scientists begin to keep a careful watch on them. On December 15, 1976, a warm ring did New England fishermen a great and unexpected favor. An oil tanker, the *Argo Merchant*, ran aground in shallow water near the fishing area. It spilled 7,700,000 gallons (29,100,000 liters) of crude oil. But the oil was trapped in a warm ring. The ring merged with the Gulf Stream and the oil was carried out into the Atlantic, away from the fishing grounds.

Like the Gulf Stream rings, the slow whirl of the Georges Bank waters traps water within the plateau. Because the water is shallow and well mixed, it is a good spawning ground for many kinds of fish and shellfish. Fish from Arctic waters, such as herring and haddock, migrate to the bank to feed. Striped bass and windowpane flounder winter there.

Of course the same swirl of water that makes a good fishing ground could also trap an oil spill from wells drilled in the area. According to Dr. Marvin Grosslein, a fisheries expert with the Woods Hole Oceanographic Institution, "strong mixing on the bank could mean an oil spill would be trapped in ocean sediments, affecting bottom life for years." Fish eggs, and the young of fish, which cannot swim away from the area, would also be killed in large numbers.

At the same time, Dr. Grosslein feels that the "crude oil would not have a long-lasting effect. But it could be catastrophic for one year."

It may sound as if he is contradicting himself. But that is not so. Dr. Grosslein thinks, on the basis of what is known about the Georges Bank and the effects of oil spills on marine life, that the fishing area could bounce back from an oil spill.

Scientists in general realize that the facts about problems like these are quite complex. In the case of the oceans, there is much that they do not know. They can advise governments and the public on the possible results of deciding to drill for oil, but they cannot furnish us with final answers. Scientists know that predictions may go

On December 15, 1976, the Argo Merchant *ran aground in shallow water off Nantucket Island. The ship spilled 7,700,000 gallons (29,100,000 liters) of oil into the area. With oil drilling in Georges Bank, such spills will certainly become more frequent.* (NOAA)

wrong—and that the ocean is full of surprises.

Science can help to guide our decision on hard problems like this one, but in the end the responsibility of deciding one way or the other is still ours.

Two things seem clear, however. It is not enough to decide a question like this one on the basis of which decision will make the most money. Also, we have to try to look ahead as far as we can—to see what our needs are and what they are likely to be in the future.

It is true, for example, that the estimated fish catch from the Georges Bank over the next twenty years would be worth about 3.3 billion dollars at current prices. The oil and gas that might be found there would be worth twice as much.

But the phrase "at current prices" shows the catch in this argument. Price is merely a reflection of how important or how needed something is at the moment. That is one reason why prices change. If the world turns out to be in need of more and more food in the future, the value of the Georges Bank as a fishing ground may soar.

On the other hand, it is true that we need new sources of energy. Yet the yield of oil from the bank—about 123 million barrels—would last us less than a week at current rates of United States oil use. Even if there were fifty times as much oil there—which is far more than the most optimistic guess—the supply would last a scant year.

Oil, once used up, can't be replaced. Fish are renewable if we take care in exploiting them, but destroy a species or a fishing ground, and it is gone.

Chapter 8 POLLUTION: MEDITERRANEAN PEACEMAKER, WORLD PROBLEM

The Mediterranean Sea is small compared to a major ocean such as the Atlantic or Pacific. It would take 101 Mediterraneans to cover the area of those two oceans.

Like the major oceans, however, the Mediterranean is an important highway for trade—and a garbage dump. Oil leaking from tankers and refineries drains into the sea. Sewage pours into the Mediterranean from millions of homes in some 120 cities along the coast. About 90 percent of the sewage is untreated, adding disease-causing bacteria to the pollutants. Wastes from factories and power plants make their own contribution to the careless deadly flood: radioactive compounds, pesticides, plastics, and toxic metals such as arsenic, mercury, and cadmium.

Partly because the Mediterranean Sea is relatively small, the effects of all this pollution are serious and highly visible. They are more serious, and certainly more visible, than they have yet become in the major oceans.

One Sea, One Law?

With 1 percent of the world's ocean surface area, the Mediterranean has 50 percent of the floating tar and oil slicks. Virus-caused hepatitis, dysentery, typhoid fever, and poliomyelitis are prevalent in many areas around the coasts of the Mediterranean. Near the French-Italian border, where there are large flower-growing areas, there are high levels of the pesticide DDT in mussels offshore.

Each year 474 billion tons (430 billion metric tons) of pollutants are added to the Mediterranean Sea. In the large open oceans, these pollutants would be spread over a vast area and greatly diluted. But the Mediterranean is almost completely closed in by land. Year after year, it loses huge quantities of water by evaporation—far more than is replaced by rainfall and rivers emptying into the sea.

As the water evaporates, the remaining surface water becomes saltier and saltier. This concentrated salt water is denser than the less salty water beneath it, so it sinks to the bottom of the Mediterranean. Water from the Atlantic Ocean flows in a strong current through the narrow Strait of Gibraltar to replace the sinking water. The current from the Atlantic into the Mediterranean is a surface current, less salty than the waters of the Mediterranean.

As the Atlantic current flows into the Mediterranean on the surface, the concentrated salt water on the Mediterranean floor flows out to the Atlantic as a bottom current. So regular are these currents that during World War II German submarines used them to slip in and out of the Mediterranean without being detected. Submarine captains simply turned off their engines and hitched a ride on the current that was going their way.

Without these two steady currents, the Mediterranean Sea would be lifeless, like the Dead Sea between Israel and Jordan. But the constant flow of less salty water into the Mediterranean and of concentrated salt water out of it keeps the sea from getting too salty to support life. And the inflow of Atlantic Ocean water makes up for the water the Mediterranean loses by evaporation. So, unlike the Dead Sea, the Mediterranean is not slowly drying up.

Equally important, the exchange between sea and ocean can flush the Mediterranean free of pollutants. But that takes a lot of time. It takes from eighty to a hundred years for the waters of the Mediterranean to be completely recycled.

The problem is that man-made pollution is pouring into the Mediterranean much faster than it can be removed by the sea-ocean exchange. By the 1970s, the pollution of the Mediterranean Sea had become obvious and worrisome to even the most casual observer.

By contrast, the world's oceans are so vast that it seems as if any amount of waste can be dumped into them and forgotten. But that is not so. The flood of wastes is beginning to leave its mark.

Sewage from coastal cities around the world pollutes offshore waters. Often it kills off or badly damages breeding groups for shrimp, oysters, mollusks, lobsters, and other valuable sea foods.

Oil from offshore wells and tanker accidents spills into

the world's oceans at an average rate of 276,000 tons (250,000 metric tons) a year. Another 1.65 million tons (1.5 million metric tons) is deliberately flushed from the holds of tankers each year. Here's why that happens.

An oil tanker delivers its cargo of crude oil to a port. Before it heads back to sea for another load, it must at least partly fill its empty oil storage tanks with seawater. If the tanks are left empty, the ship will be too light. It will ride high in the water, and this can be very dangerous on the open sea. In a severe storm, the underloaded tanker is likely to capsize.

However, the tanks can never be completely emptied of oil. A thick coating clings to the sides of the tanks. This oil-water mixture must be flushed out of the tanks as the ship nears a loading platform to make room for the new cargo. In addition, ships discharge waste oil and grease from their own machinery into the sea.

Large oil shippers now take special care to reduce this kind of pollution. One method makes use of the fact that the oil in the tank floats to the surface of the water. The water is drained slowly and carefully from the bottom of the tank until only practically pure oil remains. This oil is kept in the tank, becoming part of the new cargo.

But without strict international agreements, such care is hard to enforce at sea. Many tankers still dump when convenient.

And convenient can mean many things. In March, 1978, the tanker *Amoco Cadiz* accidentally spilled 67,000,000 gallons (253,600,000 liters) of oil off the French coast. Much of the oil washed up on French beaches, doing great damage to fish and birds. And afterward, the French nabbed several tankers dumping waste oil offshore. Clearly, the skippers of these tankers thought the oil they dumped deliberately wouldn't be noticed in the midst of a huge accidental oil spill!

Tar balls from oil spills are scattered through the Atlantic and Pacific oceans. So are bits of plastic and other floating rubbish.

Poisonous metals such as mercury and lead are dumped by industries into rivers and flow out to sea. Lead also reaches the sea from the exhaust fumes of cars that burn leaded gas. The lead is swept up into the air in the form of tiny particles and washed into the sea by rainfall. About 300,000 tons (272,000 metric tons) of lead enter the sea yearly from the United States alone.

Over the years, the mixing of ocean waters spreads pollution throughout the oceans. The oceans are so vast that the wastes are spread very thinly. As an example, that 300,000 tons of lead, spread evenly through the sea, amounts to one part of lead by weight for every five billion parts of water.

But that is enough to be a problem. Many sea plants and animals take in their food directly from the sea. The food substances they eat are, like the pollutants we've mentioned, spread very thinly through the water. So the plants and animals must be able to extract them from seawater and concentrate them in their bodies. At the same time, these living things may extract and concentrate pollutants drifting through the sea. As was mentioned earlier, shellfish feeding in waters polluted by metals such as mercury, copper, or lead will concentrate the metals in their tissues. Pound for pound, the flesh of these shellfish will contain hundreds or thousands of times as much poison as the surrounding water does.

These shellfish may poison the people who eat them. Or the poison may spread up the food chain to larger fish and birds, killing them or making them dangerous as food for people.

Pollutants from oil and pesticides such as DDT follow a similar path in the sea. So do chemicals called PCBs, used in plastics. These pollutants, too, are widespread in the oceans. They are absorbed by marine creatures along with their food.

But unlike food, they are not used up or passed out of the body. Instead, they are stored in fatty tissues and build up year after year. And as they move up the food chain, they become concentrated.

Even without being concentrated, these ocean pollutants may be a menace. Just a few parts per billion of such pollutants as oil, copper, mercury, or lead kill off large numbers of diatoms, which, as has been already mentioned, are a vital part of a good food chain that supports fish used as food by man. A decrease in the number of diatoms has occurred in recent experiments done by oceanographers from the United States, Canada, and West Germany. It also seems to be happening in the North Sea, one of the world's great fishing areas. Because of extensive drilling for oil in the North Sea, there have been frequent oil spills there in the 1960s and 1970s.

It may be years before the full effects of such repeated

oil spills show up in the North Sea, and probably little more will be done to halt or reduce them until the effects do show up. It takes a serious and obvious danger to force nations to work together on a problem such as this.

By 1978, however, the dangers in the Mediterranean Sea *were* serious and obvious enough. They brought all the Mediterranean nations except Albania together at an international meeting in Monaco, on the Mediterranean coast. The meeting's purpose was to work out some kind of agreement to control the threatening pollution of their common sea.

None of the delegates imagined that an agreement would be easy to reach. Seventeen countries surround the Mediterranean. The European states, to the north, are richer and have much more heavy industry than the African states that make up the southern coast, or the states of the Middle East at the eastern end of the Mediterranean.

So the European states cause by far the greatest part of the Mediterranean's pollution. It seemed fair that those states should bear most of the costs.

But would they? France, Italy, and Spain are the top polluters of the Mediterranean. Would these highly industrialized states sign an agreement that called for them to pay most of the price of cleaning up or of preventing future pollution, at least beyond certain limits? It did not seem likely.

And there were other disagreements. Even the poorer Mediterranean nations depend on their small industries for a good part of their incomes. Tunisia, for example, exports phosphates, which are important in making chemical fertilizers. Algeria mines mercury and lead—useful metals, but also dangerous pollutants.

These North African states and others feared that the more wealthy Mediterranean countries would use pollution controls as a weapon. They suspected that countries like France and Italy would ask that the same pollution standards be applied to all the Mediterranean nations equally. That would mean that countries with small industries would be stopped from developing them further. Meanwhile, the big industrial states would be able to keep their factories humming. They would just have to use more expensive equipment to control pollution—and they could easily afford that.

Of course, on the other side, the developed countries did not take kindly to the idea that they should have stiffer pollution controls than other nations in the area.

In fact, there was only one thing that those seventeen countries had in common. That was the Mediterranean Sea itself. If they kept on using the Mediterranean carelessly, all would be stuck with the results. If they didn't, all would benefit.

Perhaps that is why the seventeen nations *did* succeed in reaching an agreement. They agreed to cooperate in controlling sources of pollution flowing into the Mediterranean from homes and factories along the coast, and many miles inland. The treaty covers factory wastes, municipal sewage, pesticides used on crops, and fertilizers. These sources make up 85 percent of the pollution in the Mediterranean. France, Italy, and Spain have agreed to pay 90 percent of the costs. And the treaty makes allowances for differences in the size of industries among the coastal states.

The treaty, the Mediterranean Action Plan (MAP), was signed in Athens, Greece, on May 16, 1980. Under it, certain pollutants are on a black list. No factory or community in the countries signing the treaty may dump these substances into rivers or streams emptying into the Mediterranean Sea. Mercury, DDT, certain plastics, used lubricating oils, and radioactive wastes are on the black list.

In addition, there is a "gray" list, which includes zinc, copper, lead, arsenic, silver, and disease-causing microorganisms. Such microorganisms are found in untreated sewage. These substances cannot be dumped except in limited amounts in certain places and under strict controls.

Dr. Stjepan Keckes, a marine biologist from Yugoslavia, is the person most responsible for getting the MAP treaty signed. It took eight years. During that time, Dr. Keckes has been director of the regional seas department of the United Nations Environment Program. The department's job is to put together pollution control programs for eight seas around the world.

Dr. Keckes and a small group of scientists and diplomats decided to start with the Mediterranean. At times during the eight years of discussions about MAP, some of the countries involved have been at war: Arab states with Israel, and Greece with Turkey. Yet their delegates have met and talked at MAP conferences. They met because, as Dr. Keckes said, "They knew they had to act before it was too late."

When Dr. Keckes and his colleagues started work on the MAP, few believed they would succeed. Often, he was asked why they had chosen to start their work with the most difficult region—the most polluted sea bordered by many very different nations.

"Our answer," said Dr. Keckes, "was exactly for the reason that it is the most difficult region. If we succeed in that region, we might succeed everywhere.

Chapter 9 WHAT LAW FOR THE SEA?

While Dr. Keckes worked on the Mediterranean Action Plan, the entire United Nations was working to create a law of the sea. Dr. Pardo had said that the seabed was to be "the common heritage of mankind." But if so, a lot of work remained to be done. Who would be allowed to mine the seabed? How and by whom would the mining be regulated? In what way was the wealth of the seabed to be shared?

To answer these questions, the UN Conference on the Law of the Sea was created in 1973. And it was soon clear that the conference would have to wrestle with a lot of other questions as well.

The oceans are really all one ocean. We've seen examples of that fact throughout this book. What is done in one part of the ocean sooner or later has its effects on all parts of the ocean. However, the world ocean is so vast that the effects of pollution, overfishing, and other kinds of careless exploitation are slow to spread. Yet unless more care is taken, these effects are likely to become a serious threat to the lives and health of all of us on this planet.

The great blooms of algae play a vital part in restoring oxygen to the ocean waters and to the air. The ocean is becoming a more and more important source of food for our growing population. Changes in the ocean, especially in the circulation of ocean currents, can change weather and climate patterns around the world. These in turn can change growing conditions over vast tracts of farmland and perhaps disrupt our supplies of food from the land.

Most important, we know too little about how changes, natural and man-made, are likely to spread out through the ocean and multiply their effects. So the scientific advisers to the Law of the Sea Conference could only caution the delegates to make their plans with care. It would not be enough for the conference to come up with rules regulating seabed mining. It would have to deal with the resources of the sea, living and nonliving. The nations represented at the conference would have to agree on rules controlling fishing, sea farming, waste disposal and pollution, and many other problems.

In spite of this explosion of problems, the Law of the Sea conference made progress through the 1970s. The General Assembly, by a vote of 108 to 0, with fourteen countries abstaining, accepted as a guiding principle the idea that the resources of the international seabed are the common heritage of mankind. All the major powers voted for the common-heritage principle. The years of the 1970s were declared the first decade for international exploration of the oceans. And throughout the 1970s, there was strong scientific cooperation among nations in ocean exploration.

Meanwhile, the proposals for the law of the sea grew in number year by year. By 1979, the Law of the Sea Treaty contained four hundred separate articles. The number of nations working on the treaty had grown to 142. Hundreds of delegates met to work on the treaty, and they reached agreement on 90 percent of it. But, as Elliot Richardson, head of the United States delegation, said, "It's about the same as boasting that you are 90 percent of the way to the top of Mount Everest. That final 10 percent is fraught with hazard."

The questions that were hardest to decide were those with which the conference began: Who should be allowed to mine the seabed? How and by whom should the mining be regulated? How is the wealth of the seabed to be shared? For the most part, the disagreement on these questions was between the big industrial states and the so-called underdeveloped countries of the Third World.

The conference proposed an International Seabed Authority (ISA). The ISA would oversee mining operations for the UN. But how would the ISA work?

The underdeveloped countries, which made up 119 of the Law of the Sea Conference members, wanted the ISA to be an international mining company. It would harvest the mineral wealth of the sea floor and share the money earned among all nations, with more of it going to the poorest nations.

The twenty-three industrial countries, led by the

United States, insisted that such a system would not be sufficient. Seabed mining, they pointed out, would take the investment of many billions of dollars. Only private mining companies have the technology and the know-how to do an effective job of mining the seabed. These companies must be able to earn a profit on their investments. Otherwise, the companies will have no reason to put their money and their know-how to work. The industrial countries proposed that the ISA raise money from selling mining licenses to private companies. It would also get a percentage of the profits.

The two sides reached a compromise on this point. Under the compromise both private companies and state-owned companies would get licenses from the ISA. A part of the profits from this mining would be used to help run the ISA. At the same time, the ISA itself would operate a mining company known as the Enterprise. Earnings from this company would be distributed by the ISA. In distributing the earnings, the ISA would consider the interests and needs of the underdeveloped countries.

This compromise still did not get rid of the knottiest disagreement of all: How is the ISA to be run?

The underdeveloped countries wanted the decisions of the ISA to be made on the one-country, one-vote principle. Otherwise, they feared that the developed countries would run the ISA to suit themselves. In the one-country, one-vote system, the underdeveloped countries would have a clear majority.

The developed countries were just as fearful that the one-country, one-vote system would wreck any chance for efficient seabed mining. They pointed out that under such a system, the fifty-one smallest countries in the UN could run the entire show. These countries would not have much money invested in seabed mining. Nor would they have the know-how to conduct mining operations. Without the money to lose, without a direct interest in getting the metals for their own use, and without the know-how, this small group of nations might destroy the mining operations through careless or thoughtless decisions.

The underdeveloped countries rejected these arguments. Countries do not need to have an investment of money in mining or a need for the metal in order to have a stake in seeing that the mining is done efficiently, they said. As for know-how, that can be taught. The industrial countries must be willing to share their technology with the underdeveloped countries.

The industrial countries retorted that it's not so simple to teach technology. Some of the technology is the property of private companies, and the government can't just step in and take the trade secrets of the company away from it. What's more, many underdeveloped countries do not have enough people with the scientific education needed to learn these technologies.

And so the arguments went on for years. Each side has been suspicious of the other. The suspicions have considerable justification. The underdeveloped countries look back to a history of being run largely by and for the benefit of their more powerful world neighbors.

The industrial countries felt that many of the smaller underdeveloped nations have unstable and erratic governments. They have seen the governments of many such countries change hands as the result of revolutions. Often, the country is taken over by a small group of military or political leaders who claim to rule in the name of the people. The industrial nations did not want the decisions of the International Seabed Authority to be largely under the control of states whose governments may change so unpredictably.

The industrial countries had another worry as well: the danger of a war over unclear boundaries at sea.

At the start of this century, nations claimed control over waters within three miles of their coasts. Now most states claim control out to 12 miles (19.3 kilometers). Many, including the United States, claim fishing rights out to 200 miles (321.8 kilometers).

Each time countries have claimed greater control, there have been arguments among them. Sometimes the arguments have amounted to no more than angry words on both sides. Often they have gone further. Ships have been seized and crews arrested. There has been shooting.

Suppose the underdeveloped countries were to claim a 200-mile limit to their control of offshore waters. That, if enforced, would close off many parts of the seas to the free movement of ships.

Even with the 12-mile (19.3-kilometer) limit, there is the problem of international straits. A strait is a narrow waterway that connects two large bodies of water. The Strait of Gibraltar, for example, connects the Atlantic Ocean and the Mediterranean Sea. It is little more than eight miles (12.8 kilometers) across at its narrowest point. Gibraltar is just one of a number of straits that are vital to international trade.

In the past, these straits have been open to ships at all times. Under a 12-mile limit, nearly all straits would be under the control of the states that border them. Morocco, Spain, and Great Britain would all have control over the Strait of Gibraltar. The Strait of Dover, which guards the English Channel, would be subject to British and French control. Some 400,000 merchant ships pass through this important seaway each year.

Or take the Republic of Indonesia, for example. It is made up of four large islands—Borneo, Sumatra, Java, and Celebes—and approximately 3,000 smaller ones. This chain of islands extends 3,000 miles (4,827 kilometers) from Sumatra off the western coast of Malaya in Southeast Asia to the western half of New Guinea near Australia.

The islands and islets of Indonesia create a network of straits that separate the Indian Ocean from the Pacific Ocean. Indonesia lies across every major trade route between Europe and the Middle East on the one side and the Orient on the other.

There has been no problem with Gibraltar or the Strait of Dover or the many narrow seaways through Indonesia. But so long as the rights of navigation through straits are not spelled out clearly, the danger of conflict remains.

Some nations bordering on straits claim that the right to pass through a strait should be limited to "innocent passage." Traditionally, "innocent passage" applies to waters that a nation claims to control.

What does "innocent passage" mean? It is defined as passage not harmful to "the peace, good order or security" of the controlling nation. But that is a vague phrase. It can mean many different things to different nations. It can mean different things to one nation at different times.

The Strait of Tiran guards the entrance to the Red Sea. Since 1949, it has been a source of conflict in the Middle East between Israel and the Arab states that border it: Egypt, Jordan, and Saudi Arabia. The Suez Canal, controlled by Egypt, was closed to Israel. So passage through the Strait of Tiran was Israel's only direct route to East Africa and Asia. The Arab states repeatedly blockaded the strait. Finally, in 1967, Egypt used the "innocent passage" rule to deny Israeli ships the right to cross the strait. This led to the 1967 Arab-Israeli war, during which Israel seized control of strategic points along the Strait of Tiran.

More recently, the war between Iraq and Iran posed a sudden threat to the oil supplies of Western Europe, the United States, and Japan. Either Iran or Iraq might have closed the Strait of Hormuz at the entrance to the Persian Gulf. That would have cut off a major part of the world's oil supplies.

The Law of the Sea Treaty, hammered out at Geneva, Switzerland, in 1980, offered a way out of this tangle of conflicting claims for both sides. The underdeveloped countries agreed to accept a 12-mile limit to all territorial control over the sea. Within this limit, each state will have control over its coastal resources. At the same time, all states are to allow freedom for scientific research within their coastal waters. They have also agreed to a guarantee of free passage for all ships and aircraft through or over international straits.

In addition, a 200-mile "exclusive economic zone" has been recognized for each state. Within that zone each state will have the exclusive right to natural resources. That includes minerals and fishing rights.

Some states have continental shelves that extend beyond 200 miles. In such cases, their exclusive economic zone would extend out to the edge of the continental shelf.

Eventually the two sides reached a compromise on how the International Seabed Authority would be run. Decisions would be made by a thirty-six-member council. The council would represent both developed and underdeveloped countries, both countries that consume and countries that mine the minerals on the deep seabed. There would be complex rules on voting so that all interests will be protected.

Last, but not least, the nations at the Law of the Sea Conference reached agreement on fishing rights, oil and gas rights, and rules for safeguarding the environment. Pollution from ships would be carefully regulated, and ships violating the regulations would be fined. They also set up rules for the peaceful settlement of disputes among signing nations on all these subjects.

That there would be disputes, even after an agreement was reached, there could be no doubt. Creating a law of the sea that will work is an enormously difficult job. It can't be solved by setting down simple, clear, rigid rules.

Think of it as being something like making the Constitution for the United States. Like the U.S. Constitution, the law of the sea must compromise and meet as best it can the conflicting interests of many states. It must be able to change and grow as those interests change and grow.

The 180-page Law of the Sea Treaty agreed upon at the Third UN Conference on the Law of the Sea in Geneva went to the delegates of the 156 member nations for review and signing.

And then the unexpected happened.

Chapter 10 RATIFICATION OR REJECTION?

In the fall of 1980, the outlook for the proposed Law of the Sea Treaty seemed good, but by 1982 much had changed. In April of that year, 130 nations voted in favor of the treaty. Four nations voted against it. The United States was one of those four. Seventeen other countries abstained. Three months later the United States formally announced that it would not sign the treaty.

Why? In November, 1980, Ronald Reagan, a conservative Republican, was elected President of the United States. He took office on January 20, 1981. A new Congress was elected with him—a more conservative one than the country had had in many years.

The Republican party's platform on which Mr. Reagan ran for office expressed doubts about the Law of the Sea Treaty. Among other things, it said that the treaty would not safeguard the rights of United States companies to mine the seabed.

Within two months of taking power, President Reagan

dismissed the chief United States representatives to the Law of the Sea Conference and named more conservative members in their places. He told United Nations officials that the United States was far from ready to sign the treaty as it was written. He had questions about some of the treaty's provisions.

It is normal for a new President to take a close look at the policies of the outgoing administration and to make changes. This is especially true when there is a change of parties and political ideas—and there was a great change in the 1980 election.

But the work on the Law of the Sea Treaty had gone forward for seven years—under the Republicans Nixon and Ford and then under Carter, a Democrat. So the sudden action of the Reagan Administration came as a great shock to the United States diplomats who had helped to write the Law of the Sea Treaty.

But the shock waves spread beyond this country. Tommy T. B. Koh, of Singapore, the new president of the Law of the Sea Conference, said, "To demand major changes at this point would be impossible." Mr. Koh passed that belief on to James L. Malone, President Reagan's newly appointed chief of the United States delegation to the Law of the Sea Conference.

On the other hand, many officials of the five major deep-sea mining consortiums, who have pooled their know-how, equipment, and money to work together on seabed mining, were pleased with Reagan's actions. Some of these officials didn't like parts of the proposed treaty.

Among the things they objected to were:

• The production limits the treaty puts on how much can be mined from the sea each year.

• A tax system that takes a small percentage of the companies' profits and divides that money up among underdeveloped countries.

• The requirement that companies transfer their know-how to many of these same countries. The companies feared such information might include secret processes and mining techniques.

Not all mining company people agreed with these objections. One who does not is Paul Peters, an international law expert, who works for the Royal Dutch/Shell mining group, which includes both American and Dutch mining companies. Mr. Peters says that although small changes might still be possible in the treaty, "It is probably the best that can be achieved."

Meanwhile, as we have seen, the United States has passed a law allowing United States companies to register claims and apply for permits to go ahead with seabed mining in the absence of a Law of the Sea Treaty. So has West Germany. Other industrial nations are about to pass similar laws.

What these laws add up to is a kind of mini-treaty among the more powerful and wealthy nations. It will allow them to mine the seabed on their own terms.

Mr. Koh says that if that kind of "mini-treaty" goes into effect, it would not have much meaning.

But would such a mini-treaty be enough to encourage the big mining companies to mine the seabed? Oddly enough, some of the same mining people who oppose the

Law of the Sea Treaty admit that it would not be enough. Without the treaty, they feel, there will be *no* mining.

That may sound as if these people are contradicting themselves. Actually, it's a result of their looking at the problems of the treaty in two different ways.

When they demand changes, they are thinking about short-term profits. *If* they could remove some of the treaty's taxing provisions *and* keep their trade secrets *and* lay exclusive claim to seabed mining sites, they will make more money.

But then they look ahead twenty or thirty years. If the United States does not agree to a Law of the Sea Treaty, there will be conflicts about ownership of mining sites. There will be long legal arguments that will cost lots of money. And seeing these problems looming in the future, banks will not lend the mining companies the money they need *now* to go ahead.

So the tangle of conflicting interests goes on. The fight over the Law of the Sea Treaty goes on. Many diplomats, including some Americans, believe that the United States will sign the treaty before the end of the century. They think that nations that abstained in the vote—nations such as the Soviet Union, West Germany, and Great Britain—will eventually agree to the treaty, too.

We may be into the twenty-first century before we know the fate of the Law of the Sea Treaty. Yet we all must live with the consequences of whatever we do to the world ocean. So must our children and our children's children for centuries to come. The state in which we leave the world ocean will be *the common heritage of mankind.*

BIBLIOGRAPHY

BOOKS

Borgese, Elisabeth Mann. *The Drama of the Oceans*. New York: Harry N. Abrams, 1975.

Ericson, David B., and Wollin, Goesta. *The Ever-Changing Sea*. New York: Alfred A. Knopf, 1967.

Heezen, Bruce C., and Hollister, Charles D. *The Face of the Deep*. London: Oxford University Press, 1971.

Idyll, C. P. ed. *Exploring the Ocean World*. New York: Thomas Y. Crowell, 1969.

Weiss, Malcolm E. *Man Explores the Sea*. New York: Julian Messner, 1969.

ARTICLES

Anable, David. "Disappointment at Law of Sea Conference." *The Christian Science Monitor*, June 16, 1977.

"Aquaculture." *Science News*, October 27, 1979.

Armstrong, Scott. "Georges Bank: Fish vs. Fuel Feud." *The Christian Science Monitor*, November 6, 1979.

Battan, Louis J. "Protecting U.S. Stake in the Sea." *The Christian Science Monitor*, February 7, 1979.

Bibliography

"Bigger, Better *Alvin* for 18-Month Voyage." *Science News*, October 28, 1978, p. 295.

Bonatti, Enrico. "The Origin of Metal Deposits in the Oceanic Lithosphere." *Scientific American*, February 1978, pp. 54–61.

Borghese, Elisabeth Mann. "A Ten-Year Struggle for Law of the Sea." *The Center Magazine*. May/June 1977, pp. 52–62.

Borghese, Elisabeth Mann. "Shaping the Law of the Sea." *The Center Magazine*, October/November 1977, pp. 14–19.

Browne, Malcolm W. "Continuing Mexican Oil Spill Baffles Industry Experts." *The New York Times*, October 5, 1979.

Cole, John. "Scientists Gauge Extent of Recovery after an Oil Spill." *Smithsonian*, October 1979, pp. 69–76.

Cookson, Clive. "Sea Law Conference Washes over UNCSTD." *New Scientist*, July 5, 1979, p. 31.

Ehrlich, Jonathan A. "Seabed Politics and the U.S. Senate." *The Christian Science Monitor*, October 11, 1978.

"Fishermen's Future at Georges Bank." *Technology Review*, February 1977, p. 19.

Ford, Glyn, and Gibbons, Michael. "Whose Nodules Are They?" *New Scientist*, May 24, 1979, pp. 631–3.

Francis, David R. "The Broad, Deep Scope of 'Law of the Sea.' " *The Christian Science Monitor*. January 17, 1979.

"Fresh Wind for Law of Sea." *The Christian Science Monitor*, September 10, 1980.

Freudenheim, Milt. "Law of the Sea Delegates Are Close to Some Conclusions." *The New York Times*, July 22, 1979.

"Glomar Explorer Spies on Seabed Minerals." *New Scientist*, September 14, 1978, p. 748.

"Harpooning the Whalers." *New Scientist*, July 24, 1980.

Hedberg, Hollis D. "Ocean Floor Boundaries." *Science*, April 13, 1979, pp. 135–44.

Hill, Baldwin. "Getting the Drift of the Oceans Is a Major, Urgent Exploration." *The New York Times*, September 30, 1979.

Hovey, Graham. "Congress Nears Approval of Sea-Mining Legislation." *The New York Times*. June 16, 1980.

Joyce, Chris. "Seabed Mining Turns Up Few Environmental Problems." *New Scientist*, June 15, 1978, p. 733.

Loftas, Tony. "Ocean Mining Digs Up Problems." *New Scientist*, March 16, 1978, p. 710.

McKelvey, V. E. "Seabed Minerals and the Law of the Sea." *Science*, July 25, 1980, pp. 464–72.

Nossiter, Bernard D. "U.N. Setting Limits on Mining in Seabed." *The New York Times*, April 3, 1980.

Ogley, Roderick. "U.N. Digs into Seabed Problems." *New Scientist*, April 27, 1978, p. 214.

Richardson, Elliot L. "Power, Mobility and the Law of the Sea." *Foreign Affairs*, Spring 1980, pp. 902–19.

Richardson, Elliot L. "Prevention of Vessel-source Pollution: An Attainable Goal." Reprinted from *Oceans*, March/April and May/June 1980 by the Oceanic Society, pp. 2–8.

Richardson, Elliot L. "What Holds Up a Global Sea Treaty—the U.S. View." *The Christian Science Monitor*. March 28, 1979.

Ryther, John H. "Food Resources of the Sea." *The American Academy of Arts and Sciences Bulletin*, Vol. 27, February 1974, pp. 15–25.

Salisbury, David F. "A Delicate Balance." *Technology Review*, July/August 1976, p. 8.

Salpukas, Agis. "Law of the Sea Review Welcomed." *The New York Times*, April 7, 1981.

"Sea Change in World Law." *The New York Times*, April 7, 1980.

"Sea Treaty: Congress Puts an Oar In." *The Christian Science Monitor*, June 17, 1980.

Sebek, Viktor. "Whitewashing Oil Spills." *New Scientist*, March 1, 1979, pp. 668–9.

"Sewage Spill Wipes Out San Francisco Bay Fish." *The New York Times*, September 23, 1979.

Sullivan, Walter. "Drill Hole Yields Clues to Structure of Ocean Bed." *The New York Times*, July 24, 1979.

Sullivan, Walter. "Oceanographers Assess Challenges of Next 50 Years." *The New York Times*, November 2, 1980.

Sullivan, Walter. "Scientists Discover Giant Worms on Pacific's Floor Off Galapagos." *The New York Times*, March 31, 1979.

"Surprise Breakthrough in Mediterranean Cleanup." *New Scientist*, July 5, 1979, p. 3.

Swing, John Temple. "Who Will Own the Oceans?" *Foreign Affairs*, April 1976, pp. 527–46.

Tinker, Jon. "Antarctica: Towards a New Internationalism." *New Scientist*, September 13, 1979, pp. 799–801.

Van Slambrouck, Paul. "Deep-water Oil: Ocean Explorers Probe the Potential." *The Christian Science Monitor*, August 5, 1980.

Weiss, Malcolm E. "Afar—Where the Sea Floor Comes Ashore." *Science World*, September 14, 1970, pp. 6–7.

Wilkniss, Peter. "Deep Ocean Drilling—What Future?" *New Scientist*, July 6, 1978, pp. 10–12.

Wiznitzer, Louis. "U.N. Moves Closer to Ocean Treaty." *The Christian Science Monitor*, May 6, 1980.

Yanchinski, Stephanie. "Mediterranean Sea Nations Agree on Pollution Treaty." *The Christian Science Monitor*, July 18, 1980.

Yemma, John. "U.S. Trying to Guard Own Interests in Deep-Sea Mining." *The Christian Science Monitor*, June 11, 1980.

BUSINESS PUBLICATIONS

Kennecott Copper Corporation, Ocean Resources Department. "The Promise of Ocean Mining."

Westinghouse Electric Corporation. "Westinghouse Hyperbaric Test Facility."

Westinghouse Research Laboratories. "Deepstar/Searchstar Research Submersible System."

Bibliography

TRANSCRIPTS

NOVA. "Mediterranean Prospect." Copyright 1980 WGBH Educational Foundation.

Richardson, Elliot L. "Marine Scientific Research and the Law of the Sea: The Fight for Freedom of Inquiry." Lecture delivered June 1, 1979, at the Woods Hole Oceanographic Institution, Woods Hole, Massachusetts.

Richardson, Elliot L. Statement delivered August 29, 1980, to the 9th Session of the Third United Nations Conference on the Law of the Sea, in Geneva, Switzerland.

U.S. GOVERNMENT PUBLICATION

A Constitution for the Sea. Department of State Publication 8870. International Organizations and Conference Series 123. August 1976.

INDEX

Afternod (consortium), 80
Agar, 62, 64
Agassiz, Alexander, 76
Albatross (research ship), 76
Algae, 37, 38, 60, 65, 66, 98
Alginates, 62
Alginic acid, 62
Alvin (research submarine), 45, 77, 80
Amoco Cadiz (tanker), 90
Anchovies, 26, 56
Andromeda (British Navy frigate), 49
Angler fish, 30
Antarctic Ocean, 56, 57, 58
Aquaculture. *See* Sea farming
Arab states, 104
Archaeologists, marine, 14
Arctic ice pack, 40
Arctic Ocean, 19, 36, 40, 60
Argo Merchant (tanker), 84, 85
Aristotle, 15, 16
Arsenic, as pollutant, 87, 95
Atlantic Ocean
  as battleground in World War I, 41
  current from, into Mediterranean, 88, 89
  depth soundings in, 28, 43
  manganese nodules in, 78
  mountain ridge underneath, 31, 44
  North, life in, during late spring and early summer, 36
  overfishing in, 50, 52

Babylonia, 17
Bass, striped, 84
Biology, marine, 35
Bromine, 74
Brussels Maritime Conference (1853), 28, 32
Burmah Agate (tanker), 4

Cable, translatlantic, 28–29, 30
Cadmium, as pollutant, 87
Camera, deep-sea, 76–77
Cannon Shot Rule (1737), 8
Cape Cod (Mass.), Georges Bank off, 36, 82
Caribbean Sea, 4

Index

Carp, 64, 65, 68
Carrageen, 62
Ceylon moss, 64
Challenger, H.M.S., 30–31, 75, 76
China, 64, 73
Cod, 48, 49, 50, 51, 56
Cod wars, 48–49, 51
Consortiums for deep-sea mining, 79–80, 108
Continental drift, 44
Continental shelves, 44, 81, 105
Copper, as pollutant, 92, 95
Currents, ocean, 26–27, 30, 40, 41, 98

DDT, 88, 92
Dead Sea, 89
Depot of Charts and Instruments (U.S. Navy), 22
Depth of ocean, measurement of, 28, 42–43
Detection, underwater, sound systems for, 42–43, 46
Diatoms, 37–38, 39, 78, 92
Dolphins, 54
Dover, Strait of, 103
Dulse, 61

East Pacific Rise, 45, 80
Echo-sounding, 42, 43
Egypt, 104
  ancient, 13, 16
Elizabeth I of England, 17
Enterprise, company operated by ISA, 100
"Exclusive economic zone," 105

Fan kelp, 61, 62
Farming, sea. *See* Sea farming
Fire algae, 38
Fish, ocean
  kinds caught in large numbers, 56
  number of species of, 56
Fisheries, 34, 35, 36, 52, 53, 56, 57, 58, 69–70, 82, 84, 86
  and overfishing, 50, 52, 56, 69
  sound and electricity used in gathering the catch, 54–55
Flatfish, 56
Flounder, 66, 84
Food chain, 38, 56, 92
Fram (oceanographic ship), 25, 40
France, 93, 94, 103
Frank, Richard A., 82
Freedom of the seas, doctrine of, 9, 17, 18, 71
Fresh-water farming, 64, 65
Fry in nursery pond, 65

Georges Bank, 36, 81, 82, 83, 84, 86
Germany, West, 57, 109, 110
Ghana, 53–54
Gibraltar, Strait of, 88, 102–103
Gold in seawater, 43
Grand Banks, 36, 40
Great Britain, 48, 49, 50, 51, 52, 80, 103, 110
Grosslein, Marvin, 84
Grotius, Hugo, 18
Gulf of Mexico
  and Gulf Stream, 19
  oil deposits in, 81
  oil spills in, 1–5
Gulf Stream, 19, 21, 26, 27, 40, 41, 64, 82
  rings in, 82–83, 84
Gulfweed, 64

Haddock, 56, 84
Hake, 56
Hammurabi, Code of, 17
Hatshepsut, Queen, 16
Hensen, Viktor, 36
Henware, 61
Herring, 50, 51, 56, 84
Holt, E. W. L., 35
Hormones from salmon, and aquaculture, 68
Hormuz, Strait of, 104
Huxley, T. H., 34
Hydrophones, 54

Ice Age, last, 14
Iceland, 48, 49, 50, 51
Indian Ocean, 78, 103
Indonesia, 103
"Innocent passage," 103–104
International Developmental Research Centre (IDRC), 68–69
International Seabed Authority (ISA), 99, 100, 102, 105
Iodine, 62, 74
Iran-Iraq war, 104
Irish moss, 62
Israel, 89, 95, 104
Italy, 93, 94
Ivan the Terrible, 17
Ixtoc oil spill, 1, 2–4, 5–6, 7–8

Japan, 52, 57, 61, 62, 63, 64, 72, 80, 104

Keckes, Stjepan, 95, 96, 97
Kelp, 61, 62
Kennecott Consortium, 80
Koh, Tommy T. B., 108, 109
Krill, 56–58

Labrador Current, 27, 82
Laver (*Porphyra*), 59, 60, 61
Law of the Sea
  first, 11–12, 17
  need for, 11, 33
  to protect resources in the sea as the common heritage of mankind, 10, 12, 98
  UN Conference on, 97, 98, 99–101, 105, 106, 108
Law of the Sea Treaty, 99, 104–105, 106, 107–110
  objections to, by deep-sea mining consortiums, 108–109
  U.S. vote against, 107
Lead, as pollutant, 91, 92, 94, 95
Leander (British Navy frigate), 49
Life in ocean depths, 29–30

Mackerel, 52, 56
Magnesium, 74
Malone, James L., 108
Manganese nodules on ocean bottom, 75–80
Mare Liberum (Grotius), 18
Maury, Matthew Fontaine, 19–20, 27
  as author of *Physical Geography of the Sea*, 19, 26
  at Brussels Maritime Conference (1853), 28, 32
  and oceanography, 19, 25
  as superintendent of Navy's Depot of Charts and Instruments, 22–25
Mediterranean Action Plan (MAP), 95–96, 97
Mediterranean Sea, 13, 81
  current from, into Atlantic, 88, 89

pollution of, 87–88, 89, 93–95, 96
Menhaden, 55
Mercury, as pollutant, 72, 87, 92, 94
Meteor (research ship), 43, 44
Middle East, 93, 103, 104
Mid-oceanic Ridge, 31, 44
Mimosa (freighter), 4
Minimata disease, 72
Mining, deep-sea, of minerals
consortiums for, 79–80, 108–110
Law of the Sea proposals for, 99–102
"Mini-treaty" for, 109
problems involved in, 79–81
Mussels, and aquaculture, 68–69

Nansen, Fridtjof, 40
National, S.S., 36
National Oceanic and Atmospheric Administration (NOAA), 6, 82
Naval Observatory (Washington, D.C.), 24
Navigation, 20
Navy
British, 28, 30, 49, 51
United States, 19, 20, 22, 28
Nile River, 16
Nodules, manganese, 75–80
North Atlantic Drift, 40
North Sea, 35, 50, 52, 92, 93
Nursery pond, 65

Ocean Management Inc. (OMI), 79, 80
Ocean Minerals Company, 79–80
Ocean Mining Associates, 79
Oceanography, 19, 25, 41
Oil deposits, undersea, 1–2, 81–82, 86
Oil spills, 1–7, 84–85, 88, 89–91, 92–93
wildlife threatened by, 6–7
Overfishing, 50, 52, 56, 69, 97
Oysters
and aquaculture, 61, 68
pollution of, 71–72

Pacific Ocean, 103
manganese nodules in, 77, 78
overfishing in, 52
Pardo, Arvid, 9, 10, 97
PCBs, as pollutants, 92
Peru Current, 27
Peters, Paul, 109
Phoenicians, 16
Physical Geography of the Sea, The (Maury), 19, 26
Plankton, 36, 38, 39, 52, 64, 65
Pliny the Elder, 15, 16
Pollution
of Mediterranean Sea, 87–88, 89, 93–96
from oil tankers, 90
from poisonous metals, 72, 87, 91–92
of sea foods, 89
Porphyra (laver), 59, 60–61

Reagan, Ronald, 107, 108
Red Sea, 16, 38, 104
Richardson, Elliot, 99
Rifts in ocean, 44, 45, 80
Rings in Gulf Stream, 82–83, 84
Robinson, John, 6, 7
Ryther, John, 66, 69

Salmon 56, 68
Salt from seawater, 73

Sardines, 52, 53, 56
Schneider, Eric, 7
Sea farming, 59–61, 63, 64, 65, 66, 68, 70, 71
Seaweeds, 60, 61, 62, 64, 66, 74
Shellfish, 61, 84
  pollution of, 72, 91–92
Shrimp, 54, 61
Soviet Union, 10, 11, 46, 52, 55, 57, 62, 110
Spain, 80, 93, 94, 103
Stone Age, 13, 14
Straits, international, problem of, 102–103
Submarines, 41, 45, 46, 88
Suez Canal, 104

Territorial sea, 8
Thor (Icelandic Coast Guard boat), 49
Tiran, Strait of, 104
Trawlers, 33–34, 54, 55
Trout, and aquaculture, 67
Tuna, 52, 56

United Nations, 9, 10, 80
  Environment Program of, 95
  and ISA, 99
  and Law of the Sea Conference, 97, 98, 99–101, 105, 106, 108
United States
  delegates to Law of the Sea Conference, 99, 107–108
  in treaty to bar weapons from seabed, 10–11
  200-mile (321.8-kilometer) zone around home waters of, 51–52, 102
  underwater detectors built by, 46
  and underwater oil-drilling sites, leasing of, 81–82

"Vacuum-cleaner" method of deep-sea mining, 79, 80
Vine kelp, 62

West African states, fishing rights of, 53–54
Whales, 38, 54
Woods Hole Oceanographic Institution (Mass.), 66, 84